In Memory Of

Crystal Pinkston
Jan. 2, 1974 - Feb. 25, 2004

Stupid Boy

Stupid Boy

Rodd Brown

ZONE PRESS
Denton, Texas

Stupid Boy
Rodd Brown

No part of this book may be reproduced or transmitted in any form or by any means, graphic, electronic, or mechanical, including photocopying, recording, taping, or by any information storage retrieval system, without the permission in writing from the publisher.

Although the author and publisher have made every effort to ensure the accuracy and completeness of information contained in this book, we assume no responsibility for errors, inaccuracies, omissions, or any inconsistency herein. Any discredit to people, places or organizations is unintentional, but some names have been changed and some facts altered to protect the innocent.

© 2007 by Rodd Brown

Published in the United States of America
By Zone Press
an imprint of Rogers Publishing and Consulting, Inc.
201 North Austin
Denton, Texas 76201
info@zonepress.com

Dr. Jim O. Rogers, Editor

ISBN: 0-9777558-8-6

CONTENTS

Prologue	7
My Guardian Angel and Me	9
Crystal's Tragic Death	17
Innocence Lost: Childhood	23
Father's Day: Arrogant SOB!	37
The Salesman: Domestic Ass!	41
Balloon Man: Angry as Hell!	63
Twilight: FBI Raid	71
Jigsaw Man: The Addict	85
Worn Out: Sentenced	103
In Shock: The Inmate	117
Daddy, Father: Which One?	127
Next Stop: Halfway House	137
Rock Bottom: Hurricane Katrina	147
The Fight: Born Again	161
God and Rodd: The Ministry	173
Epilogue	181
Acknowledgements	189

To those still suffering and/or in recovery

Prologue

Writing this book is not easy, because it is another step in becoming real, admitting my failings and owning up to what God wants me to be. Sharing these stories and lessons learned is not about me telling other people what's wrong with how they live. It's a story I see around me a thousand times every day. I just don't want other people to suffer the way I suffered or run away anymore from the ways I made other people suffer. I don't ever want to go on hurting people. If I stay silent, then that is just what I may be doing.

My life story is not always a forgiving story. Truth is a hard teacher. The truth is I cannot write a book forgiving how I've acted. Yet, at the end, I hope you'll see it is a story of forgiveness.

There was another price and, looking back, only God's grace could have let me face it and survive. When my criminal defense lawyers were working out a deal, either for house arrest or to get me out of a long prison sentence, my old way of living and lying would have said "I did it again! I got a deal!" I would have convinced myself that even in losing I was winning. You'll see how God moved a false promise of time under house arrest into something far more difficult. My prison sentence could have been the death of me since at that time in my life I was suicidal and certainly capable. I wondered just how God could have turned his back on me and risked my life?

These dangerous delusions were shattered by all the crimes and wrongs I had done to the people who loved me. Without God, my recovery would have never happened and the love my family has been able to provide, would no longer exist.

For those of you who are suffering, I say this:

You can't remake your life alone. You need God's help to turn it around. For a long while I thought I'd been abandoned by God; but the ugly truth is I had abandoned God. I knew I was doing things that made me ashamed to the core of my soul. I kept telling myself that I could handle anything and everything alone. I made a terrible hell of my life by trying to live without God. When I decided I needed help and asked for it, God was there for me. He'll be there for you, too, my friend. All you need to do is ask. And to think my pride nearly killed me, you ***stupid boy***.

My Guardian Angel and Me

This is a story about me and there is an angel involved. I tend to believe it is my guardian angel. Many of us have guardian angels who protect and watch over us. These angels were once living and breathing people, as we all are right now and strangely enough, our own guardians are often complete strangers. We never knew them during our lives and now we find them surrounding and protecting us while holding our hands through our own ongoing battles.

It may seem crazy to some. Guardian angels? Sure. Before my own encounter, I would have thought the same thing. Guardian angels are for psychics at the local strip mall.

"Twenty bucks and I'll tell you your future! Twenty-five and I'll introduce you to your guardian angel!" They cry out as I come near. I pass them on by, rolling my eyes at their slew of psychic charms and items for sale. I've seen it too many times to fall for such a thing. Guardian angels . . . Ha!

The believers are given air time on daytime television, Oprah, Geraldo, Montel. Where these stars pay even more expensive psychics, just to introduce people in the audience to their angels. Even the (perhaps) more reputable prime time shows such as Dateline and 60 Minutes have had segments on the belief in guardian angels. I remember finding it funny. It wasn't long ago that I would watch those shows with people who had "been to the other side," or "seen the light," and I would scoff. Those terms are so ingrained into our social psyches that even the youngest of children know what they mean. It's commonplace to talk about death and life after death; but to believe? To really believe? I wouldn't have thought so.

That was all before Crystal, my own guardian angel.

The spring of 2004 brought with it crisis, as in two weeks I was about to be sentenced to federal prison for healthcare fraud, not to mention that I was fresh out of two drug treatment facilities and another divorce; and yet I still found myself dangerously addicted to prescription pills. I was a proud person but mentally suicidal. I like to think my pride was too strong to end my own life.

I was an outcast to those whom I once called friends and family. Those who dared to enter my circle stayed an arm's length away, a safe distance. Rumors followed me of wiretaps and microphones. Those who spoke to me did so with a tight tongue, never sure how far away (or close) the feds were. At one point it had been leaked that I was offered leniency for an exchange of names. Everyone was very careful when they spoke to me with buttoned-down lips, as they over analyzed their own words. They spoke in as few words as possible, never mentioning business, corporations, or money. Everything around me was scrutinized, if not by the Federal government, then by my own friends and family. It was hard to realize that I was no longer the person they had known. In their eyes, I had been revealed. Yet I wasn't the rat they thought I was and I had no intention of being that person.

So if everyone assumed I was being tightly watched, they were right. I was being watched by the local authorities, the feds; and worst of all, by my loved ones.

Denton, Texas, is a small town that takes pride in it's uniquely diverse and creative community. It's the quality of life that many feel separates this small town from the biggest of the Texas cities. With a pervasive music culture and two major universities, the small town has the feel of a relaxed and young environment hidden from the crime and turbulence of the big city. In fact, prior to me, the only other time federal authorities had been involved in Denton was in the seventies, when a rancher just north of Denton had spent some time in a federal prison for tax evasion. But, time forgets most wounds and he has since moved on, to Wyoming or Idaho, with a small herd of cattle to settle down with.

Now it was me, public enemy number one.

Looking back, I think it was fate that Crystal chose to protect me. I was virtually homeless and so I drove into the city that morning needing something, although not quite sure what it was. Actually, I needed my Dad, if nothing else than to just see his face. He was so strong to me, such a powerful figure, that just a reassuring glance from him would have served it's purpose.

I drove my car into the parking lot of my Dad's office that day. He was outside, simply sitting in a chair staring out beyond me and to what, I had no idea. He took himself away from his thoughts long enough to notice me but nothing more.

This would be one of the hardest things I had ever done. Pride had always prevented me from ever loving or accepting love and that morning would be new for me. Not only was I looking for someone to love but also someone to love me back.

He gave me no attention as I walked up to him. My body shook. First, I had no money, which meant no pills and my body had already started to react to the withdrawal and the ten years of addiction. Second, I was afraid. I had no idea what to expect. Before me sat a man who had been hurt by his son. He had loved everyone in his life with an amazing passion and now was facing the reality of not being able to love his own son. He was also the man, unbeknownst to me, who had just the night before been given the sage advice, "Never give up on your children!"

Through this angelic advice, I found out later, Crystal was suddenly alive!

It was a very tense and long few seconds as I walked up to him. I felt like a gunfighter crunching my boots into the hardened ground along the main street. The fear, the anticipation and the sadness of not knowing what would happen. It was the result of years of self-satisfying lack of growth, where the only person who mattered to me, was me.

"Here are my keys." I said.

He looked at me, for the first time since I arrived, he looked right at me. "What do you want me to do with them?"

"I need help."

"What do you mean?"

I pulled an empty pill bottle from my pocket and tossed it to him. The shake in my body was still uncontrollable but I had to do it. "I want to kick these drugs," I said.

His eyes winced and began to water slightly and I wasn't sure if it was relief, anger or sheer frustration that caused the tears. Nevertheless, Dad sat there before me, six feet tall and two hundred and fifty pounds, wounded and visibly shaken like I had never seen him before. He wiped the tears away with the broad side of his forearm.

"This is hard on me and your mother," he said looking toward me, his lip quivering helplessly. He had been through hell because of me and sadly, I brought more with me that morning.

"I know."

"I really don't know what I can do." He tore his stare from me and shifted his eyes away, back into the largely empty parking lot.

"Help me, please."

"What makes this different from all of the other times?"

"It just is."

Dad gripped his fingers into a very tight ball, bowed his head and begged, "Dear God, give me strength and courage to do the right thing."

Dad stood up and then staggered toward me. He was tired and very weary but he chose not to abandon me that morning, which looking back, was a divine intervention, no question.

What I have written here was the beginning and end of sorts, for a twenty-year journey. This was the turning that would begin a long and tedious process of healing and spirituality, taking me places and dealing me consequences I had never prepared for.

What happened in my life was very painful, very special and could only have been written by the hand of God. I slowly began the painstaking process of loving others more than myself. More importantly, I stood still long enough to hear the cries of God's voice.

I have assembled the following narrative exactly as it happened so perhaps, through this story you can find hope and truly understand a family's unconditional love for their son and brother. And what is most important, the relentless pursuit of a very forgiving and loving God.

You may not believe in guardian angels but for this story and the fact that I didn't commit suicide or flee the country while living in an emotional abyss, you can dismiss any and all preconceived notions. This angel is faith-based and sent directly from God.

Although Crystal died a very violent and bloody death during a home invasion gone terribly wrong and with her baby in her arms, that morning with my father, she was the most beautiful angel ever descended from heaven.

Crystal gave my dad strength that morning to give me one more, last chance, which absolutely saved my life. With a sigh of relief and strength, Dad made a few calls to my Mom and brothers, Scott and Todd, to tell them what was happening. Against all odds, we set sail to begin our new journey together. Public enemy number one, his dad and God.

Crystal's Tragic Death

It had only been three days since the final chapter of Crystal's life came into focus; the tragic final days. Jacked up on years of rage and emotional instability, she had lost her parental and visitation rights to her little girl, Cierra. It was too much for Crystal. It would be too much for any mother who loved her daughter. A short time later, emotions and rage played another role in her final hours as she made her way to her daughter's daycare and without a second thought, she took Cierra. She kidnapped her own daughter and fled.

For several hours, Crystal locked herself away in a mobile home. She had a pistol in one hand as the Denton County Police circled and cordoned off the area. She was no longer merely kidnapping her daughter. Crystal was now playing for life and death. Crystal was now entering into a dangerous standoff with the police and negotiations were going nowhere. She was scared and her mind must have been in chaos. The police began to sense they had to do something and in an aggressive maneuver to resolve the situation without incident, they decided to send in two officers through the mobile home's side windows. They knew Crystal didn't want to hurt her daughter and hoped that she would merely desist once she had seen there was no way out. After all, she was just scared.

Both officers made it safely into the home and positioned themselves for the confrontation. They would meet her somewhere in the middle but then things went wrong.

Crystal heard a noise and gripped her daughter more tightly. She was disoriented as the police came at her from both sides. With her daughter in hand she began to swing her pistol in the air above her head, her finger on the trigger.

"Get out of here!" She screamed. "Leave me alone!"

Then Crystal pointed her gun at one of the officers and fired. It missed him and within seconds, everything was over. The one shot from Crystal sparked crossfire between the officers. Crystal had been shot several times in the head, killing her instantly. Her lifeless body collapsed to the floor as a pool of blood slowly began to form around her.

From outside, hysteria broke out as Crystal's mother and friends could hear the screams of the baby following the gunshots. Nobody knew for sure what happened as they began to cry out and hold each other, fearing the worse.

Crystal's life had ended and sadly, this was the same outcome that I increasingly thought would eventually bring peace in my own life.

The night of Crystal's funeral, Dad called Crystal's mother, Debi Blagg, to offer his condolences. They had been longtime friends and Dad needed to offer his love and support to Debi. He offered Debi the use of his RV for any friends or family who might be in from out of town. It was vintage Dale Brown. My father.

They talked a very long hour and with Debi aware of Dad's own problems with me, she offered advice to my father, advice she wished she had learned another way, lessons she was learning first hand. Debi asked my father not to give up on me. She asked my father to support his children and be there when they needed him the most and never to give up regardless of the circumstances.

Later, after I learned of this conversation, I communicated with Debi, because I knew her contact with my dad helped her. I also told Debi that her being guided to open up to my father had ultimately saved my life.

Debi,

I know you have been through hell but your decision to talk to my dad is the reason I am alive and able to share my story. In crossing each other's paths, daily, we demonstrate how miracles work. For your loss, I am so very sorry. For your intervention, my heart will forever sing a song of peace and praise for you. I think

Crystal was serving as my guardian angel through you on such a cold day of despair.

My path has been anything but easy. I expect it will have many bumps along the way but I am here for the long haul, to heal myself and to let you know that you are not alone in your desire to find your gifts, to make difficult decisions to better your life and to re-embrace the love that surrounds you, with open arms and open hearts.

In Christ,
Rodd

Debi wrote me, a comforting message that still brings me strength to go on whenever I feel at the end of my rope, over and over.

Rodd,
I am quite saddened by Crystal's loss and the events that occurred from her taking Cierra to the ending of Crystal's life. I will never understand why she was so mutilated. She was a beautiful and wonderful person and I miss our movie nights, midnight shopping at Wal-Mart, just acting silly and enjoying life. That I truly miss. I rejoice in her new complete life as she was a Christian without doubt. I am thankful she is no longer hurting.

May God continue to bless you. You and your Dad are definitely the chosen ones. I love you both. You have made my heart sing

and put a smile on my face without tears.
God has given me the strength and courage.
I know without a doubt Crystal is rejoicing in
heaven at your recovery.
Blessings always,
Debi

If as you read this, you are in the midst of an addiction, an abandonment by a loved one, a death, uncontrollable anger, criminal behavior or any other human failing, it's time to sit still long enough to listen to God's voice. He will speak to you in these times, there is no doubt. It's whether you listen to His message that will determine the rest of your life.

Chapter 1

Innocence Lost: Childhood

When we are children, we are taught to dream, to use our imaginations in a way that will help us to grow. From the moment our parents respond in delight at our first words, we are seeking approval. In my own journey, I discovered many subtle ways in which childhood innocence is lost and approval is perverted.

I became infected with ambition and desires of greatness that had no real purpose other than to gloat triumphantly with my success and to lord it over everyone else. While ambition is not a bad thing, we should all want to improve ourselves and our situations as we grow. We need to recognize those from whom we are seeking approval. I accumulated a lot of wealth; most of it dishonestly and without the intent to spend it on my family or to make a difference through charitable works. It was just a way of feeding my own ego.

Of course, I never wanted anyone to know my life was based on a lie. I wanted many others to see what a success I was, to hear praise from my brothers and my parents, especially my dad who was so hard to measure up to, with his own real success.

But in fact, as so many had suspicions all along and I finally realized after an FBI raid, loss of my medical equipment empire, going on welfare, drug rehab, divorce, federal prison, halfway house and ultimately homeless, it was all one big lie.

Summer, 1977

My youth. It was an era of new experimentation for youth. Drugs were easy to get and many were adhering to Timothy Leary's advise of,"Drop out, turn on and tune in." Before it had been daring to smoke and drink. Now there was marijuana, cocaine and still an abundance of drinking and smoking, albeit more conventional weeds.

Every ten or twenty years, things change radically from the "good old days." I grew up in the 1970's, when sex and drugs went with a generation gap and Watergate. Changes in society should never be an excuse but I am emphasizing that the choices I was making did not make my parents very happy. I'm not being honest enough there. My choices began to make my parents miserable. Where some kids get away with a hand in the cookie jar, I wanted the whole jar.

My dad represented the values of the earlier generation but he was incredibly well-known and well-liked in our town. He wore his conservatism lightly and was popular in all social circles. My dad was the Willard Scott of Denton. He was the jovial, cheerful personality that was irresistible and highly respected, not just for his wealth but because he was a man everyone could relate to. It made you feel good just to be around him.

My dad was a blue-collar success story, an ambassador to mankind, starting out with next to nothing and fulfilling the American dream of earning and working his way to wealth. He worked hard and he played hard and he was always ready to help a neighbor, or even a stranger, in distress. Over time he became one of our town's leading citizens, willing to listen to the problems people brought him, ready to provide counsel and wise advice.

Dad owned Brown and Brown Body Shop, an operation that maintained almost celebrity status for thirty years. Men of all ages and occupations gathered at the shop in the mornings before daybreak to drink coffee, tell stories, laugh and talk professional football and, in the latter years, NASCAR. The shop was very magical, almost mystical to me, my brothers and to others in the community, as well. There was just something about the way my dad did everything, from managing his business to managing people, that made it special.

My dad was larger than life, nicknamed "Delwynn" by our great family friend, Michael Hart. Nicknames are often one man's way of showing brotherhood, love, respect, admiration and many other aspects that represent a bond and friendship. My dad was no exception. There were many who had given him other nicknames along the way. There were: "Brownie," "Kippy," "Big Boy," "Brown Bugger," and several others that come to mind but for some reason the name, Delwynn, just stuck. Long before "A-Rod," "T-Mac," "Stone Cold," "Prime Time," "The Playmaker," "The Worm," "Pudge," and "The Donald," there was "Delwynn." It became his nickname for life.

My dad was always the life of the party. He laughed louder and deeper than others. His jokes were funnier than the ones everyone else told, or maybe it was the way he told them that set him apart. He always seemed to stand taller and prouder than those around him. Dad was proud but never arrogant. Even to this day I wonder how he manages to keep a sense of balance between the admiration of those around him and his own inner sense of place in the world. He is very proud of being Dale Brown but not nearly as much as everyone else is proud of knowing him. He walks with a confidence that lends itself to total control, a man who always knows where he's going and what his purpose is.

From the early days, Brown and Brown Body Shop produced enough money for our family to have a stable lifestyle; but my dad went above and beyond merely producing an adequate income to provide for his three sons. Almost by accident, he entered the rental property business in the late sixties and never looked back. My grandfather had developed a new neighborhood in north Denton and naturally built a new home for our family. Mom and Dad moved to the new house but couldn't find a buyer for our old one. Worrying about the extra liability, Dad rented our former home. That was the first of dozens of income-producing rental homes he purchased throughout the years. From the mid-1980s when he was really at the top of his game, he took on the apartment complexes, building his own complex near the campus of North Texas State University (now The University of North Texas). What Dad started as an investment out of necessity became a money maker for our family. It was the rental money that provided all the extras we were blessed with over the years; a lake house on Moss Lake, jet skis, multiple boats, cars and trucks. By the time my twin brother Todd and I turned fifteen, we had regular vacations and a new Cadillac every year for Mom. Of course, Dad always had a new Suburban in the latest color and style. That was back in the good old days, when Suburbans were "Carry-alls." I can still hear my dad exhorting Todd and me to do things for his latest vehicle.

"Go get in the Carry-All!"

"Clean the Carry-All!"

"I'll be waiting for y'all in the Carry-All!"

To us boys, the Carry-All was the most magical vehicle ever built. Mom, of course, had different ideas. To her, the best car was always a Cadillac Coupe De Ville.

Todd and I, along with our older brother Scott, had our own toys, thanks to Dad's income. We had motorcycles, go-carts, bicycles, unicycles, skateboards, billiards, pinball machines, anything and everything. Were we spoiled? By things? Yes. By our parents? No. Life as a Brown boy was incredibly good, Scott, Todd and I agreed. As so many other families back then wondered about whether their families loved them, we didn't have to wonder. We knew we were wanted and loved.

Looking back, there was far more to his wealth than a ton of money, which as a child, it's hard to see. Only as a teenager did I first begin to notice how hard Dad worked. The long days, juggling money and the stress he was under as he worked to ensure our welfare and prosperity. Even when I didn't live up to his expectations, I respected him and what he stood for and I unconsciously absorbed his ethic of hard work and the importance of putting others at ease, wanting the respect and admiration of my peers as he had from his own generation.

Unfortunately, as I continued to grow up, I didn't absorb the central lesson of his success, that it came from honesty in all his dealings and in the compassion he had for those around him, those less fortunate than he was. Dad could always be counted on for help when an individual or a family was down on it's luck. He was a good listener to the problems of others and always took the time to listen, rather than being quick to give advice off the top of his head.

Dad was a "man's man" as defined by his own generation. He smoked cigars, drank a lot and came across as someone who could be counted on absolutely to meet his obligations, both moral and financial, in the community and at home. He believed a man had a responsibility to take care of his family and to help in his community as well. To me, my dad was the sun, the moon and the stars all rolled into one. I expected

I'd be just like him when I grew to manhood. That was before I realized I had been well started down my own, very wrong, disastrous path.

My mom was the perfect complement to my dad's personality and way of life, one of the true Proverbs 31 women in the world. She was the perfect stay-at-home mother. There is a saying that behind every good man is a good woman and there is no question that is true in my dad's life. My mom was and is, his strength. My parents' lives were a childhood romance that carried over into their adult lives. They started dating when they were in the eighth grade. In high school, Dad was captain of the high school football team and Mom was the Homecoming Queen. That set the tone of their life long love affair. Their love story is one for the ages. They have loved one another unconditionally through all the trials and tribulations they have faced, many of which, I'm sorry to say, were caused by me as the years passed.

Their love has withstood events that would crumble most marriages. They've been best friends since the day they met and it still amazes me the way they still honor and admire each other after all these years. Mom jokes that Granny and Granddad didn't like my dad and she giggles and jokes, saying that she should have taken their advice! Whenever Mom brings that subject up, Dad always looks at her with his little puppy dog face and says, "Oh, is that right, Mrs. Brown?"

In so many ways, their love, so rooted in the Lord, is a model of innocence. No, I'm not saying ignorance but an innocent belief in doing the right things, for the right reasons.

If Dad made Brown and Brown a wonderful workplace, Mom made our home simply magical. She has a knack for decorating and our home has always reflected this. Once we kids had all graduated high school, she began her own, very successful interior design firm. Our home was always decorated in the latest trendy colors. The seventies were all about yellow, orange and green. The eighties were more about earth tones, brown, yellow and orange. You could tell the decade by the appearance of our home.

Unlike many families today, where kids have to forage for bowls of cold cereal for breakfast, Mom cooked breakfast every day before we went to school. She got up each morning to heat the stove and cook a warm meal. Even when it was something as simple as French toast, we all loved breakfast. She cooked a fresh meal every single night, when Dad didn't man the grill on the patio. We always ate together as a family each night at six. When the dinner hour approached, my dad would simply whistle for me and Todd to come running and we'd run back home like a couple of Lab retrievers eager for food.

At the table, we blessed the food.

God is great,
God is good,
Let us thank Him for our food. Amen.

We ate like warriors filling up before marching into battle, with Dad at one end of the table, Mom to his right, Scott at the opposite end, then Todd, since he was left-handed and me next to Dad's other side. We discussed the day's events and, of course, we all ate from a large bag of Fritos and at least two pickles each. Fritos and pickles were the first form of organized religion I can remember.

As for growing up in the Brown home, it was just like Mayberry. Everything was very magical and I look back on those years with true delight and a sense of splendor.

Holidays were absolutely the best part. Mom decorated the house from top to bottom. During Christmas, our house was more brilliant than the North Pole! We lived the American family dream in an amazing and wonderful environment. As for drinking, Dad was wealthy and it was the thing for his generation to do. Drinking was en vogue, as was smoking cigars and cigarettes. My dad came home each night around 5:15, made his way immediately to the bar in the game room and poured himself anything alcoholic and water, though usually Cutty Sark or Wellers. He then would make his way poolside and begin drinking and smoking. He always had at least three glasses of whiskey every night but not once, ever, did I see my Dad drunk or out of control. Perhaps, on his "buttocks" as Forrest Gump would say but that was well deserved and not liquor-related.

So, if Dad drank back then the way most men did, it was cool and calming and a relaxing way to end the day. Being on top financially in the seventies certainly cleared the path for Dad to do whatever he wanted to at the end of the day. He smoked Swisher Sweets in the house, with all the attendant odor! I remember the day I tested my own manhood and bought a package of Swisher Sweets. I literally turned Pappa Smurf blue and was throwing up all over the yard. It wasn't until several years later I learned one isn't supposed to inhale cigar smoke. My lungs and entire breathing system were in recovery for several months following the fiasco. For all his business success, Dad was a functioning alcoholic. Mom was a social drinker. It was the way people in their generation acted. It was the norm and they were in no way an exception to that standard.

Alcohol was the legal drug of choice for my mom and dad's generation. It was the era of social drinking at parties and even at home. Drinking was an acceptable way to lubricate any gathering. Later, young people began to experiment with other chemical substances, many of them mind altering and I wasn't immune to these opportunities. No one saw anything wrong with heavy alcohol consumption. In many circles a man's ability to hold his liquor without becoming harsh or abusive was considered a sign of manliness. My generation interpreted this as a sign that it was okay to drink and to try other drugs as well. In a way, we kids became enablers for our parents, by silently adopting their social norms.

In high school, I played the part of "preppy bad boy" with wealthy parents. Like many kids with too much time and money, I began experimenting with alcohol and was soon on the way to becoming an alcoholic. Not even eighteen, I had already picked up my first addiction. Children of privilege often find themselves enjoying the easy availability of alcohol at home and with more money than sense, teenagers

stjude.org

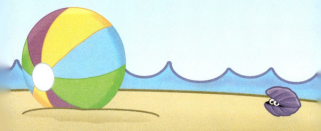

usually could find it available away from home for a price. I was no exception. Drugs were the 'in' thing to do-party with friends, Todd and I were no exception.

College should be a time of exciting and expanding opportunities, to decide on what to do with your life but I saw college as a place for expanded partying. I had no clear educational goals. College was simply the place I went after high school and I planned to enjoy it's excesses to the max. It wasn't hard to find a group of students with the same (lack of) aim and I was soon introduced to a new level of expensive fun, one that included cocaine as well as alcohol. I started college at the beginning of summer, on the Monday after my graduation from high school. My first college venture was over soon after.

By the end of that summer, I was home again after flunking out of college. Now began my junior college circuit years, where I drifted from one school to another, continuing to party, acquiring DUI's and becoming involved, often disastrously, with a series of young women, before finally settling in at The University of North Texas and focusing on completing college.

I started to take college seriously only when my friends from high school were graduating from college. I had nothing to show for those years but degrees of partying. The partying slowed down but only until I achieved my degree. No way was I going to be shown up by other people. I was still doing so many of the right things, for all the wrong reasons. So, by my standards, I'd finally accomplished something important and it was now time to show the world I could succeed.

Jobs weren't very plentiful the year of my college graduation and while I was more than willing to be an all-star executive and start at the top, the reality is I had to settle for a dreary start as a used car salesman. But I made a great success of it, earning bigger commissions than my established peers. Using my success and budding confidence, within a year, I was employed at a major medical equipment company, once more reaping successes in sales. The success was almost as intoxicating as drugs and alcohol and it left me tense and anxious, leading to new chemical dependencies to alternately quell anxiety and feel that I could do anything. I married a beautiful woman. I made lots of money. Best of all, for my ego and me, I soon founded my own company. It was a reflection of all I wanted to be. Ever read Dorian Grey? It's a book about a man who appeared eternally young and handsome; but an enchanted portrait showed the rot in his soul. Like Dorian Grey, I tried to keep my true portrait shrouded. I figured I could cover the bets, too

As I've learned.

God loves everyone, so a Christian should too. In fact, Jesus said that the most important thing in life is to love God with everything we have and love others as we love ourselves. While the advice to love others as ourselves may seem strange since many people tend to equate love of self as a form of vanity or pride, Jesus knew that the person who has very low self-esteem and thinks he can't be worthwhile won't be able to see those around him as lovable either. Loving oneself, in the best sense, is accepting that we're children of God, with a divine heritage of his love, that we are loved by God and have the potential and power to be the people God wants us to be.

It is not always easy to love everyone around us, is it? Sometimes we strongly disagree with other people's political views, religious beliefs, behaviors, favorite teams or foods and it makes it hard to love them when we feel like we're right and they're so very wrong. But Jesus doesn't separate loving God and loving others. Maybe the best way for us to show our love for God is actually by loving other people no matter how hard it can sometimes be. In fact, it's the only way.

Sadly, some of us have never loved or been loved because our addictions and chaotic worlds won't allow it. To truly feel love for the first time in my life, even when it's been there all along, is the most amazing feeling in the world. I know I'm loved and I love, because my parents stood by me, battled the whole enabler thing and never stopped loving me. I now understand and feel love. Love is the most powerful emotion you will ever feel and I pray that you can find it by opening your heart to it's possibility. There are plenty of people waiting to love you, if you'll only let them. I can certainly testify this to be true in my life!

When God finally did deliver me, there were hundreds of people who didn't believe it and for very good reason. When God converted me, he converted a monster. If you are on the front end of your conversion or walk with God, let others say whatever they will about you, you know you're on the right path. You can't get mad at your critics, blame them, or argue whether they're right or wrong about you. The best way to show them you have changed is to keep walking by faith, keep on the right path and let God handle other people and their opinions. In fact, this is the most powerful witness you can have. Be glad others are watching! Show them God through your changes. For those like me, it may take months or years (or even never) before others truly accept that you've changed. Your walk with God is about you and God, nobody else. Get the 'you and God' part straight first and everything else will follow. Trust me. I've tried everything else first and it didn't work.

When we do things with a purpose to please God, we begin to feel confident being in our own shoes without needing the approval of our neighbors, co-workers, or family. Oddly enough, when we stand tall in our faith and our actions reflect that, the approval of others comes in droves, without effort and is far more rewarding.

Chapter 2

Father's Day: Arrogant SOB!

All through the 1990s, I was on top of my world. I could do anything, buy anything, use and manipulate anyone to get what I wanted but I was paying for the exhilaration I felt. My drive for more, more, more was turning into an anxiety to go higher, feel more, do it all. I began to take Klonopin, a powerful tranquilizer meant only for small dosages over a week or two (not as I did, for ten years), as my drug of choice but often used many others such as Valium, Oxycontin and Xanax. While deciding to rid myself of a cocaine habit, I just traded one drug for another. Then again, wasn't I always making deals?

My childhood home was faith-centered but my heart was not. I was taught that God loves us all. For as long as I can remember, I knew that my life held a purpose much grander than I could ever imagine. However, early in my journey, I somehow feared that this purpose would keep me from living the lifestyle I dreamed of having. You see, parents often forget that their kids have their own ideas on the most adult pursuits. When I heard about someone following the path God set forth for them, it was usually a path of living by humble means without the trappings of wealth. Not for me. As a result, I made choices very early on that took me farther from my purpose and farther and farther away from God.

I had become a wanderer without any anchor in my life. We all have gypsy souls if we continue to pursue life without God. We will always turn out miserable, discontented and without purpose or direction. For a time, it seems easy to just "go with the flow," accepting whatever new thing happens, agreeing to the way others see us. If we make a huge mess of our lives, we must be worthless. Right? If everyone thinks we're bad, evil, utterly without hope, they must be correct. Right?

Wrong! God knows the truth. We each have a divine purpose. We can change. We have someone who loves us, who trusts in our ability to be a force for good even when everyone around us says we're worthless failures. God will always be there for us, loving us and encouraging us to change, to cleanse our souls of doubt, self-hatred and pain.

Many of us on the Earth believe we have ultimately blown it in our personal attempts to fix our lives. Empty, meaningless rituals of society seduce us and I am no exception. As you read this book, there's a good chance you'll conclude no one could have been as wrong-headed as I was. If so, then learn from my mistakes.

We have all tried at some time to find peace in

ourselves without God. The hedonists blow it because they are pleasure-centered and not God-centered. The judgmentalists blow it because they are high-minded and not God-minded. The legalists blow it because they are work-driven and not grace-driven. I had blown it because it was all about Rodd, not God. Nowadays, the labels we apply in religion are getting to be just as useful as the bar codes on everything we buy. They tell us how much but never how good, something really is.

We spend our lives consumed in finding contentment outside of Jesus Christ. Are we super-sizing our contentment in our misery? Like me, too many people are, as the wise adage says,

Buying things we don't need
With money we ain't got
To impress people we don't even know!

Of course, I was busy trying to buy the people who loved me, too.

Summer, 1998

It's Father's Day and to my credit, I haven't made an ass of myself. Only because it was still early in the day. I'm cruising to work in my Dodge Viper, resting my other toys; the Escalade, BMW and Big Dog, feeling as confident as can be. Driving a piece of machinery such as a Viper sure gives a man the moxie to approach the world with an extra dose of me attitude. Funny thing, a lot of people sure give a lot of bowing to these shows!

For me, it will be just another day at the office. There will be cheating, intimidation, cussing, a high level of screaming and more than likely a tantrum or two (if any of my previous stuff didn't qualify) but there would be money made and, in my mind, I would be the only guy making that happen. For the fraud that I was, I waved a certain flag of integrity in the fact that I employed people and provided them a good living. There is a responsibility in that concept that I took seriously, at some level. Unfortunately, the pool reflecting this virtue was a very shallow one.

My cell phone rang.

"Hello," I said answering the cell phone with one hand, sipping coffee and steering the Dodge Viper with the other.

It was my mom, who invariably starts every sentence off with my responsibilities, "Well, did you call and wish your father a Happy Father's Day?"

"No."

"Are you going to?" While this is a completely fair question, it shaves a bit rough on the ears since I probably would have blown it off assuming that he knows I love him and that I am busy. She knew me then and still does know me, better than anyone, so she was simply keeping me in check. But that hadn't been working since I was thirteen.

"Of course," I said, smashing the turn signal with my left hand. The Viper is terribly cumbersome to drive but I bought it for the image and really could have cared less if it drove like a corn plough.

"Todd and Scott have already called him. I just didn't want you to forget."

"Thanks Mom."
"Well, how's everything else?"
"Fine, just working."
"Did you get moved into your new building?"
"Not yet."
"Why?"
"Contracts. Dotted lines. You know the deal."
"Yeah, I know the deal," she mumbled in her own little way.

I offered to come by for dinner. This would appease the situation and if for some reason I got hung up, of course everyone would understand. As we talked about the details, a better idea was to meet somewhere else for dinner. This was always a great opportunity for me to show my family how much I loved them. Yank out my cards, flash the cash, no holding back when you were out with me and there would certainly be no holding back for my father on Father's Day. "How about the Roadhouse?" The Roadhouse was a barbeque joint in Argyle. It was a very old school with it's raw wood, wagon wheels, deer heads, large mouth bass and antique guns. It was a good place to unwind.

We said a few more things before hanging up. I turned the radio on and continued toward my office. I shifted gears and felt that awesome feeling of going fast. The coffee was cool enough to gulp down, so I did. As you can see, I like things to happen fast, even my coffee. At I-30, I had this burning desire to go East, towards Dallas. I shifted through more gears and passed cars. As the wind blew through my hair, the music was at top volume and I was one cocky guy. It was good to be Rodd Brown, or so I thought.

In the midst of reveling in my own personal glory, I noticed a Dale Earnhardt truck on the opposite side of the road, sitting on the used car lot of Don Davis. I immediately exited and made my way back around. After all, it was Father's Day, my dad loves NASCAR and I hadn't bought a gift, yet. This was a perfect truck. It's tires were brand new and ready for off-roading. The rims were shiny and screamed expensive. The paint scheme screamed, "Look at me!" with fancy MR. GOODWRENCH decals plastered all over the head and quarter panels. The Dale Earnhardt signature was above both doors. The roll bar was the perfect final touch on a perfect truck.

I made my way into the driveway to begin impressing the hell out of everyone. I started to step out of the car. "How much?" I asked as I pointed to the truck before I had even unwrapped myself from the Viper.

A very large, balding man with bling on at least six fingers swaggered through the parking lot. His shirt was tucked haphazardly and he breathed very heavily. Of course, he had the 'Mont Blanc' pen in his shirt pocket. He was willing and ready to make a deal. "It's on sale today for only $22, 000! Best deal in Texas!"

"$22,000 huh?"

"Yes sir. One of kind."

This was exactly what I needed, a one of a kind, $22,000 Father's Day gift for my dad. I would sit back and watch everyone's reaction and how they would gleam at all the love I showered upon him.

I! Me! Rodd Brown!

It would be a beautiful sight, one that I was sure would bring a tear to my mom's eyes. This is hard to admit. But it's true; there was a price tag on showing my love and everyone would be so proud of me. My delusions grew bigger and bigger.

I played several scenarios over in my head while 'Boss Hogg' circled the truck. He and I were partners in the ego crime and working very well together. I would give him his first sale of the week and he would supply me with more food for the ego. We were a match made in heaven.

"You take cash?"

"Well, hell yes, we take cash!"

"Good. I have plenty!"

"How do you like the Viper?"

"Oh, it's a toy," I said with a smile.

"A toy, huh? You gonna make this truck a toy, too?"

"This is for my dad."

"Your dad?"

"Yes. Father's Day."

"Let's walk inside and buy your dad this truck, wadda' ya say?"

Hogg walked as if he had won the Super Bowl. Back and forth. Back and forth. His arms swayed mightily. He sat me in his tiny office, bragged of a few plaques he had won over the years, his kids, his wife, then began scratching out a contract.

One hour later, I was the proud new owner of the Number 3, pitch black, Dale Earnhardt Silverado. I drove that truck around for a few minutes, since I never even bothered sitting in it before buying it. I was honking the horn and waving.

I couldn't wait to show my dad, then everyone else!

At a few minutes before six, I arrived at the Roadhouse with Dad's new gift. He and mom were already there so I parked the truck at the perfect angle, then swaggered into the restaurant.

"Come see your gift," I said to my dad as I walked towards their table.

Instinct overcame him and I could sense his fears. Still, I was confident that this would be something he would cherish forever. I opened the restaurant door with a smile as big as Texas across my stupid face. There it was!

My father, in his early sixties, was a humble man who knew what a healthy self-ego was made of. Mine was certainly not healthy and well out of control. As the truck was exposed, my father was literally in shock. This truck was not something he needed or even wanted. I was simply imposing my arrogance upon him. My father driving this truck would be one great big billboard for me, a huge symbol of what a great son I was and how successful I had become. He was now forced to wear his son's arrogance, as if either of us needed it. My father certainly didn't care about it.

The truck would be parked. It would be forgotten.

As I've learned.

I was so out of control trying to impress others that I eventually found an amazing peace in prison. I remember sitting in my cell, having this tremendous amount of peace! For the first time since college, only in prison would I eventually begin to accept me for who I was and it was the most awesome beginning I have ever experienced. A paradigm shift occurred for me in that I completely changed the way I was thinking about myself, my role in the world and how I affected others!

What a time to remember my childhood, in prison but that's one of the things I did, later. I imagined being able to know then, what I knew now. When I lay idle in prison on many of those lonely nights, staring at the ceiling, my head on the top of the green, plastic pillow with the one sheet and a thin blanket gathered across my chest, I wondered what in the world happened to all those people I was trying to impress. Not one of them ever really liked me for who I was. They were only impressed with the superficial items they could quantify, how much money I had, how big my business was, how expensive the car I drove was. Even then, most people probably weren't too terribly impressed beyond a passing fancy. That is exactly why not one of them was around when my world collapsed. Had they taken me for who I was, I thought bitterly, they would have been able to accept me for my mistakes, just as Jesus does. I can't blame them however, because I wouldn't have been too impressed with me either. The fact is there was no "me" there for them to know. If anyone had the guts to tell me what I was and what I was doing, I would have tried to destroy them.

I realized in prison the need for inner peace. When you have this, people will jump on board to fight to the death with you. You will never be able to buy that loyalty, however much money you have. When it's all said and done, you're the one you live with. So it's about acceptance. God already accepts you. If you can accept God's love and then accept yourself, you will never be alone.

Chapter 3

The Salesman: Domestic Ass!

Of all I have gone through, writing about my marriage is the hardest. I'm not going to sugarcoat this story of my marriage for anyone. Not even for me. Besides, what we do in our married life says the most about what we have done with our living. It was my life, it's who I had become. The final outcome is in the miracle that God created in my life. For a long time, I lied to myself, to my wife and to God to keep the ugly truths away, that I was responsible for the downfall of my marriage. I tried to hide the monster I became.

I have been married three times. Twice to the same woman (Cari) who is the mother of my children. As a husband, I was a provider only in the strictest material sense of the term. I put a roof over us, filled our home with beautiful things to keep Cari 'satisfied.' Now it's painfully obvious to me I certainly was not providing any of the love and support she deserved in a marriage. From my twisted point of view, I needed to keep her 'happy' (translate, 'quiet') because without her, there would be no one keeping a watchful eye on all that I had earned. Without her, the neighbors would have questioned the perfect world I built. If I couldn't keep my wife in line, the world would see I didn't have a wife who adored lovable me.

So I had a perfect wife, a strikingly beautiful woman but I was far from the perfect husband. Strange as it seems, Cari and I get along well now (even though we have our differences). In fact, far better than couples who have gone through much less and while there are many reasons for the peace between us now, three stand out. First, we choose not to 'win' if we disagree but rather talk it out. Second, we realize our daughters need both of us. Third and most importantly, God delivered me and Cari no longer has to deal with a monster. It's pretty obvious God heals a lot of people when He heals one person.

Let's start with the obvious. Marriage is a very hard institution, even when the times are mostly good and when the couple loves and respects each other. It's an even harder institution when the husband is me or someone like me. For years, I was angry, controlling, anxious, self-consumed, unappreciative, abusive, loud, obnoxious and too proud to ever let a woman into my life as a partner. I met and married Cari in 1999 and never gave the marriage a fair shake. Beyond the anger, we had sex the first night we met. She became pregnant within the first five days.

We were like care free children playing house. We were giddy, running around like a couple of kids. I had just bought a home in Grapevine, Texas, before meeting Cari. She was struck with my charisma and my money. I know, because I used money like flypaper. I used wealth as a way of convincing people I was good, loyal and caring. I was struck with her amazing beauty. We both convinced each other it was a match made in heaven, at first. I was about to turn it into a hell for both of us.

Cari and I were sort of a romantic set-up, the original blind date, from the beginning. My company was hiring and interviewing and I interviewed Kelly, a friend of Cari's. Kelly told Cari about the job opportunity and more than that, about me. So, we arranged an 'interview.' When Cari walked in that morning, she was the most beautiful woman I had ever seen. Naturally dark complexion. Tall. Brown eyes. Brown hair. I remember she was wearing a black dress and had a barbed-wire tattoo on her shoulder.

After the interview, we went to lunch and that night we saw the Rangers play the Yankees. The evening should have ended there but it didn't. We spent the night in bed together and so our affair began. After she told me of the pregnancy, I became the true Rodd Brown. I immediately denied the baby was mine. I was screaming, yelling, cussing....

"You bitch! You whore! White trash! Dumb ass!"

Then I went on about her family, her mom, her dad and her brother. No insult was too small for me to hurl at her. Ironically, all of her family was to be there for me after the FBI raid. In fact, her dad, Stan, was the most loyal father-in-law a man could ever want. Stan is a very successful business man. After the raid, he loaned me more than $50,000. He was very patient with me. Kind. Always opened his house to me and yet when Cari and I fought, I was very quick to bring him up as one more of a family of losers. Was I thinking straight? Obviously not.

I was a very sick man and if you ever bring up the in-laws in an argument, you too, are a very sick person and if you yell at your wife like I did, you are mortally ill.

I insisted she have sonogram after sonogram, making sure those doctors pinpointed the exact day and time of conception. Cari was in a relationship right before me, so I began using that card, suggesting the baby belonged to her former lover. I was finally asked not to attend any of the doctors' appointments with Cari. Then, toward the end of the pregnancy, Cari was ordered to bed rest. How many of her problems during pregnancy were brought on by me? It's difficult to say in retrospect. I was already making her life hell and our daughter was yet to be born. The fact I was kept away from her stressful medical care suggests the fact I was poison.

After Cari gave birth to our first child, we moved a few miles to Southlake. We played our parts, mere roles in a play that we called our married life. I've already said marriage is referred to as an institution and you were probably hit by my ironic use of the term. After all, prison is an institution, too and I think I now understand the difference. Cari and I were using our marriage as a means of scaling the social ladder, no different than if we had paid a ton of money to get a country club membership to show society all we had accomplished and to make ourselves a part of the "happily-married" club. My role as a husband was far from healthy, right from the start and it only got worse as time went on. I snipped at Cari over the least little thing, arguing over big things, little things and nothing at all.

Cari is a very good woman. I took advantage of that by manipulating and abusing her emotionally and mentally. When you play the game of fraud as well as I do, you become quick at finding people's hot buttons and you punch them over and over until the person gives you what you want. Cari was no exception. In fact, since we were intimate, it was much easier for me to toy with her to gain the upper hand. Withholding sex was her way of regaining some of that control, to maintain her own sense of dignity. She had me and she knew it and I gave her everything in the world; except what she probably really needed and truly deserved, a compassionate partner who respected everything about her. Instead, I abused her thoughts, feelings, love and then her body.

We met and married for all the wrong reasons and God was nowhere to be found. Sex was the only language we used for communication and we never learned any other. Then when sex was gone, we had nothing to talk about. I never bothered learning who Cari really was. I was clueless when it came to understanding her feelings, aspirations, desires, goals, needs, wants or fears. It was all about me! Everything in my life was about the show and my marriage was no different. So while I could say that she never tried to understand my feelings, I think she had valid reasons for shunting them aside. After all, my feelings changed with the wind based on my addictions.

I was so overwhelmed with being Rodd Brown that she simply grew tired of looking for the real me; the one she wanted to have children with. My attitude was that it was my life and she should be thankful to be a part of it!

I truly believed only in me. It was all about me; and Cari was only a pretty accent to my life.

Before our first child was born, we became more like roommates than spouses. She did her things as a woman and I did mine as a man. We made our public displays as required for our social status but little more. When things got rough, we argued. The honeymoon was over and we had never established healthy lines of communication and I probably never could have, by then. Not without asking for help.

Fall, 1999

"Not today!" Cari said.

"What is wrong with you?"

"Just not interested," she said, pulling a cup from the cupboard.

When she was hard for me to get, Cari was the most desirable woman I had ever seen in my life. Her exotic looks were accentuated by her dark hair, caramel complexion and deep dark eyes. Aside from having a perfect body, she knew exactly how to accessorize, from the clothes she wore to the navel ring and barbed wire tattoo on her left shoulder. Yes, I found my wife very attractive. She had a natural sex appeal to her.

Cari was wearing her typical workout clothes, ready to leave for kickboxing and I was wearing khaki shorts, a Dallas Cowboys tee shirt, flip flops and a UNT hat worn backwards.

So, there I stood, wondering what it was going to take to get my wife interested in ditching her workout to spend the day with me. It was a beautiful Saturday morning and my beautiful wife in our beautiful home had zero interest in me. This wasn't the first time we were arguing about sex, yet, peculiarly, we were still newlyweds. She was in her twenties and I was in my early thirties and there was no sign that I would be able to express my love to my wife on this day, or at least how I thought I was supposed to express my love.

"What do you mean, not interested?" I asked, trying to find some angle.

"Not in the mood. Not today. Maybe tomorrow."

"Tomorrow?"

"Yes."

"How many other guys have to deal with this crap!"

"One for sure."

Now keep in mind that I controlled everyone around me. I was an expert at sales and manipulation. Yet here I was unable to sell my wife on my concept of doing what two people who supposedly love each other do. I made my way toward her, setting up a sale.

"Baby, you know I love you."

"And I love you," she said with a tight voice.

"Why don't we wait and see, huh?" Cari would usually acquiesce to my needs verbally, simply to get me off her back and nerves. "We'll see."

I had made progress but there was little chance that this would happen. It didn't take long for Cari to see me for what I was after. I guess to people outside my grasp it was always apparent but she lived with me, so she saw the darkest sides my psyche could produce.

"Wanna meet for lunch?" I continued to probe.

"I suppose."

"How about Chili's at noon?"

"I hate that place."

This was going to be a tough sale. Wasn't she supposed to be in love with me? We were newlyweds. What was the problem? The problem was that I had already shown Cari she was nothing more than an object in my world of making many acquisitions. For being made to feel like she was a prize, not a woman with feelings and needs, I was being given a cold shoulder more and more often.

We argued over the place to have lunch and both our tempers flared. We were no longer fighting about having sex, we were fighting over the inane subject of lunch. The conversation was on the brink of being verbally abusive. Very. There was no holding back with Cari and myself. When we fought, we fought to win, with scores, rallies, volleys, smashes, points, extra points, field goals, home runs, grand slams and bottom lines. Compromise wasn't a word we had ever discussed, not once. She learned very quickly that compromising with me would mean compromising to me. She'd have to give in on everything, always. So it was all or nothing. This had become the nature of our volatile relationship.

On several occasions over the next few months, the cops arrived to settle the score. Twice, I made that lonely trip to the downtown police station, handcuffed and cussing. This morning, I practically stalked her as we spoke, keeping myself as the buffer between Cari and the phone. All I wanted was to be with my wife and now I was trying to prevent an altercation. Or more accurately, her reporting one.

"What do you want, Rodd?"

"To have a normal relationship. That's it."

"We have never been normal." Her tone was flat and forlorn.

Sadly, she was correct, not even the day we met was an exception. I've mentioned some of it. Within twenty-four hours of meeting we had gone to lunch, gone to the Rangers' game, gotten drunk, bought her out of her apartment lease, bought her a BMW, moved her into my house and had sex, over and over again. Finally, we had fallen asleep, then woke up with more sex followed by a break with breakfast and then more sex. Feelings were never discussed; they really never seemed like an issue. In retrospect, this sorry beginning to our marriage was to be a key in understanding my immature and insecure drives to dominate.

Consistently, that day I was determined to get my way. "Why are you always mad?" I asked, trying to get my 'sale' by opening her up, by playing with her values and her head.

"Mad?" she inquired, surprised.

What I didn't realize was that I was going to get a lot of answers I didn't want to hear. Cari would bluntly share things with me that would only make our relationship even more antagonistic from that point on. She knew I was a sham; she knew everyone who wasn't afraid of me saw me as a sham and she was about to tell me that she knew. There was no way this scene could end positively.

"You beat me up verbally to the point of not wanting sex. Physically! Emotionally! Mentally! Then you drag me to church every Sunday so we can look like the rest of those hypocrites!"

"Just go have . . ." I was done.

"You drive me absolutely crazy! You trapped me with your lies and money and now I'm stuck!"

Of course, at this point, it made sense to me to just get rid of my problem. I told her to go back to her parents. She obviously didn't like me and didn't want to be with me. It made no sense for us to be together but for some reason she stayed. When I really think about it, there are several reasons that she probably stayed. The first was the tremendous mind twist I put on her. The next was pride. How could she really tell everyone that she was wrong about me and they were dead right in their assessment that I was utterly no good?

"I should've listened to my parents in the first place," she almost whispered. "They told me not to marry you! They said you were no good!"

She was about to call me for all that I was, which really meant she was about to tell me that I really wasn't much at all. She likened me to an old boss of hers who had killed himself when his greed and misgivings caught up to him. This is 1999, long before the heat started breathing down my neck. Of course, at that moment, the idea of me being caught seemed funny. I laughed off the chances of getting caught. Of course I would never get caught, let alone kill myself. Looking back, I didn't know she was so crystal-ball right. I was killing myself. First, though, I killed off Cari's love.

Know that when you throw money around to show off, you should realize most people stick around and are your friends because of the money. It's not really because they like you or think you're anything special. You're just buying their time, not their respect. Cari knew this. I may have been a great salesman but she was much more in tune with the human pulse than I was. Although people probably rarely said things directly to her, she was well aware we were already a joke in the community and there is nothing more that a person in denial hates than when someone knows their secrets. Secrets they are so desperately trying to hide, even from themselves. Cari knew all of my secrets and my failings; and apparently, as I was to find out harshly, so did everyone else.

Cari was convinced that if I didn't end up killing myself, I would make enough enemies along the way to have someone do me the honor.

"Then someone will hurt you! You're just a mean person!" She got the last word before she slammed the door to the garage. "And forget lunch!" Even raging, Cari was still Cari.

Cari was correct in so many other ways. Yes, I

did eventually get to such a point of self-loathing I seriously considered killing myself. She was also right in seeing that I was trying to be the most self-centered human on earth. I hurt Cari, deeply. It truly breaks my heart to know that I did all that to a great human being. It took me being a year out of prison before she would even speak my name.

Cari was a survivor. I was a coward.

Sunday mornings I would pack up the car with my wife and daughter, dressed in our Sunday best to give praise to God. In church, I leave the girls in their pew as I publicly show my faith by administering communion. I proudly stand there addressing each person, with the power of denying them the body of our Lord Jesus Christ. "Body of Christ," I say as I judge them, knowing they hold their own dirty secrets and wonder if they know about mine.

After church, the appearance of love is rampant and like a swarm of bees, we congregate sharing unfeeling hugs and dominant hand shakes. Finally, I gather my family after demonstrating to God and the world how much I love and thank Him. We pile in the car and head out for something to eat. In the process, my wife and I are unable to agree and the righteous man I was just ten minutes earlier, judging others in their path to salvation, we fight. Not only do we fight but the language that spews from my mouth and the names I chose to refer to my wife at this moment in front of our daughter are beyond inappropriate. They are abusive and painful. I know I am not alone in this behavior. Have we just been bottling up our anger by acting so pious and spiritual?

As I've learned.

I was good at hiding things. I even tried to hide what I had become from God but I can no longer do that, thanks to His saving grace in my life.

It took a long time for me to realize some sad truths about my marriage. One, I destroyed my family. My wife and kids were simply drained by the experience. Two, my baby girls had to endure a hell I created. Three, I sold my wife Cari the lie that I was the kind of man I wanted her to believe I was. She fought like hell to keep us together, when most women would have thrown in the towel a lot sooner and walked away. Cari has an amazing strength, which she demonstrated throughout our marriage. When all was said and done, she was beaten down almost to the point of no return. And hard as it was for her, I am very proud of the mother she has been to our daughters. Most of the time during our marriage and afterward, she had to be both mother and father to our daughters, because I was not fit to be a father for many years.

It is no wonder that our kids are confused. Mixed messages are coming at our youth from every direction. Go to church and be good but please ignore the scandal of rampant sexual abuse by the priests. Do your homework and all your chores but Mommy is going to drink herself silly at Bunko because Daddy abandoned us when you were a baby. Drugs are bad but it's okay for Daddy to take a hit from a joint, so long as he doesn't get caught.

What we are teaching our children is that there are standards set for different people, where different rules apply. We are teaching our children to be the hypocrites venomously chastised by Jesus in the Bible. We are not teaching this simply by what we say but instead, by how our words contradict what we do. As parents, we have the most important job that can exist, to mold our children into healthy, functioning, contributing members of society. We lay blame on others because our children's misdirection can certainly never, in our own minds, be our own fault.

There is a wonderful movie called Two Brothers, about two tiger cubs separated as cubs when their father is killed. Eventually, their mother is hunted and both cubs are domesticated in different homes, one with love and nurturing and one as a threatening killer. The film is a beautiful reflection of life and parenting. The father dies trying to protect his young cub. The mother tiger, while protecting their second cub, is hunted as a result of her efforts to rescue the first brother lost. Eventually, the two cub brothers are held as pets and eventually pitted against each other, in a gladiator-like duel as adult tigers. In realizing their own blood kinship, they turn this death duel into play field, rejoicing in their reunion. Watching something as dangerous as a tiger naturally causes duress in the crowd. Not seeing the tigers fight each other causes a panic. How I can relate! In the chaos, the brothers escape, fleeing the hunt and return to their parent, deep in the jungle, where they will finally learn to hunt and live according to their natural calling. We must fight for our children no less than the mother fighting to find her cub. We must find our natural calling and be true to it and above all, we must "Love your brother!"

This true love of brethren is something much

deeper than saying, "I love you". This is something much deeper than buying someone a big present, such as a truck. Real love is seen through our daily actions to demonstrate our love. Love is in the continuing respect toward someone's opinion, when we don't necessarily agree with what they are saying. Loving your brother, or sister, or mother, or father, or neighbor, for that matter, is about constantly placing their needs as a priority. This isn't to say that you should always sacrifice your needs or desires but instead always to try to understand how your actions play a role in other's lives and with that knowledge, adjusting your needs and desires and game plan accordingly. Unfortunately, too many of us learn this by hurting other people. Then, when we're alone, we feel the probing voice of conscience, or God. One reason I'm writing so frankly in this book is to plead with any reader in a similar situation to really listen to what caused my loss. If one person stops and saves the love in their marriage, this is more than enough for the pain it causes me to recall those dark times.

Cari tried hard to stick by me in my darkest days. Cari stayed in the aftermath of the raid and the loss of our home but at last could take no more. Eventually I lost not only my home but also my wife and children. Finally I had to face what I had done to create a personal hell for myself and my family in marriage. A failed second marriage with Cari turned out no better- in some ways, worse-because I had not changed. I still wanted to be on top of the world at whatever cost to my loved ones and myself. She actually tried again! What a love to have lost.

All too often, a couple mistakes physical attraction and lust for love, which can only be enduring if it grows over time as the couple gets to know one another, discover they have similar values, want the same kind of things from life. Their lives need to be God-centered, not focused on themselves. No marriage begins or continues perfectly. But for a husband and wife to find true happiness, each needs to care more about the feelings and needs of their partner more than their own.

I know I've learned this lesson in my life so that my next marriage and I pray I'll have one, will focus on honesty, caring, commitment and on solving problems together rather than creating new problems by myself. Truly, a marriage is a marriage of minds as much as bodies, where we learn to love one another and cherish one another so that we can at last learn to catch just a glimpse of God's love for us. A good marriage is a reflection in the greatest sense of that divine love our Creator bestows on us in which we truly learn to love one another as we love ourselves.

I always believed women were my downfall. Actually, it was me demanding them how to love me, more and more, that became my downfall, since I had always taken God out of every relationship. I wanted them to love me as I loved me and that, my friends, was my downfall. Why should anyone love me to death?

Chapter 4
Balloon Man: Angry as Hell!

As the pressures in my life mounted, all the goodness in me was squelched deeper and deeper. Drugs played a role, alcohol played a role but my ego was the star. One problem with ego is it's full of hot air. Ego is a balloon and even as it gets bigger and bigger and bigger, the most fragile ego you can have is a big ego. A big ego always gets popped.

My ego was so fragile to any wind of change or challenge, that I used force to get my points across. It was such a problem in me, that it is still a struggle for me. Our emotions are like a poison, if we don't process them in a healthy way. I was in a constant state of fury, demanding instant compliance with my whims at the office and at home. As I weakened, through drugs and then crime, people finally started to fight back.

Though I didn't realize it at the time, people were around me simply because of the money. My employees didn't respect me. My business associates were fed up with my antics. Any friends in my life were hanging on by a thread, my family simply tolerated me and sadly, this included my wife. She lived with the most egotistical, self-absorbed type of bastard in the world; a rich drug addict. The fact that she called the police only twice about my violent behavior is simply mind-boggling. In short, I thought the world was staging a rebellion against me just by virtue of my being alive!

As egomaniacs, we do not want to give up control. It is not one of our attributes. We tend to do things in panic, haste and anger to maintain control at all costs. I was no exception.

Fall, 2000

On an August morning in 2000, I had a meeting with Don Myers from Sun Medical, a medical equipment company based in New Mexico. I had been dealing with them for years and didn't mince words. I arrived at the office and, as usual, made my way into my office without saying a word. How you enter any room first determines the control you can have over people. The simplest control is fear. I understood this implicitly. All my staff feared what might come out of my mouth at any given moment. This fear I instilled in them was my way of maintaining my position as "king." My financial reports sat perfectly aligned at the corner of my desk for my scrutiny. At this point in the fraudulent scheme, it was all about the money.

Oddly, my kingdom had already begun to crumble. I was absolutely in denial about this being even a remote possibility. Just like the gambler who thinks his bad streak is about to end, I threw those dice every day, again and again, confident that things would be looking up soon. My winning streak would resume. In reality, most mornings were spent shuffling money and deciding which bills to pay. Things were about to get worse.

When someone tapped on my office door, I barked a, "Come in!" already frustrated with the numbers I was looking at on a spreadsheet.

"Sorry to bother you," Polly said in her broken English. She was from Laos, a country in the southern tip of Asia and she'd been in the United States for six years. Polly sat in one of the two chairs across from my desk. She crossed her legs and arranged some small, yellow papers in her hand. I considered Polly my right hand. She knew me better than I knew myself and she had an amazing way of defusing my black moods. Even so, like all the others in my life, she also walked on pins and needles every moment of every day at the office.

"We have a problem with an order," she informed me, sharing the guilt for something that had gone wrong. "Remember those chairs you ordered from Don a few weeks ago? I think they were the wrong ones."

"What do you mean, 'the wrong ones'?" I tried to say in control. My patience was gone at this point. I was stretched so far financially that one wrong order could put me under.

Polly took a deep breath, "You ordered K-11s, right?" K-11 was a code used to bill Medicare for power wheelchairs and K-11's offered me one of my highest 'returns on investment,' based on standard billing. I could purchase a power chair for $1,000 and through K-11 billing, be reimbursed from Medicare $5,000. Naturally, I was adamant about billing each chair as a K-11 expense. My company offered no other models simply because there wasn't enough profit in them and Polly was very aware of this policy.

I pulled the chair closer to my desk and slammed my hands down. "Then what's the problem?" I looked her dead in the eye.

"Don't get mad, please," Polly pleaded.

"What's the problem, damnit!" My voice was rising, getting louder and more threatening.

"They were K-12s," she confessed.

"What!" I leapt from my chair and began pacing around the room. I crammed my hands in my pockets, then pulled out my keys and threw them at the wall. I knew it was a huge mistake, financially, since we had already billed Medicare for the K-11s. "Have we already been paid?"

My mind raced as I confirmed the facts available to us. Someone would pay for this mistake and it sure wasn't going to be me. But I needed to have all the information before I sent my unlucky staff member to the firing squad. Then I decided on a course of action, in my anger, that would start a chain reaction which would finally bring the walls around me crashing down.

"Get Don Myers on the phone immediately!" I ordered.

"But . . ." Polly started.

"I don't want to hear it! Get him on the phone! Now!" I was bent on instilling the fear of God in Polly that she'd better move fast or she'd have to deal with me. Polly hustled to get Don on the phone.

The mistake was worth well over $100,000.00 and I wanted answers. Don would certainly fix things because I was a big client. In my mind, there was no way anyone could fail to want to be associated with me. Was I ever wrong!

I was on the brink of self-incrimination and had no idea of the results to come from my actions. I wasn't just angry, it was beyond that. People who knew me always said 'anger' wasn't nearly enough to describe my emotions. Fury, maybe. My associates said anger was just too tame a word, something more was needed, a word with more evil intent, malice and meaning. It was a running joke within the company, perhaps everyone's own little way of somehow adding humor to a very vicious man. Some might say rage would fit but that might be glossing it over as well. How do you describe a potential hurricane as bad weather?

"Rodd . . ." Polly muffled through the intercom on the phone.

"What!" I barked as if she was still disobeying me, when all she was doing was telling me that my request had been filled. Don Myers was on the phone.

"What in the hell's going on, Don?" I demanded.

"We made a mistake," Don said mildly.

"A freakin' mistake? What do you mean a mistake?" All I really wanted to know was what he was going to do about it.

"I am not going to let you talk to me like that," he

shot back.

"What are you going to do, hang up?" I challenged him.

"Yes," Don stated matter-of-factly.

"I will get you fired, you moron!"

"Rodd, I'm serious," Don replied, irritated at my outburst.

"You freakin' coward! I'll fly out there and whip your ass!"

Click.

There's a very old joke that goes, where does a giant gorilla sleep? Anywhere he wants to. That morning, I was the giant gorilla, on a rampage, I was ready to show the world I could do anything I wanted to in my territory. I jumped up from my chair and stalked into the main office area. I began stomping my feet, yelling at everyone in the office. I bent over each desk, veins bulging, face red while I screamed and cursed and pointed a finger of blame at anyone and everyone. I might be a giant gorilla but, looking back, I'm sure I behaved much like a four-year-old in a tantrum.

I back-handed everything from Debbie's desk, then Polly's, Angela's, Sherry's and Barbara's desk. There were papers scattered everywhere.

"Turn off that god damned music!" I screamed, pointing at the radio.

When no one jumped fast enough, I yanked the radio's plug from the wall. The radio music kept right on pouring out its cheerful tune. It was operating on batteries. "Shut up!" I yelled at the radio, then threw it at a wall. The employees all ducked. They had seen some of this before but each time I lost my temper, it was getting worse.

A tyrant, I laid my royal path through the office for the next few minutes. I grabbed filing cabinets and began yanking out drawers. Everything was fair game in my ranting destruction. After all, it was my empire and I could do whatever I wanted.

"I hate this place! Fuck every one of y'all!" I ranted as I went. Finally, my rage spent, I stalked to my office.

Back in my leather chair, I took a deep breath. For a few long minutes, I just took panting breaths. It was all I could do. As usual and well beyond the anger, my mood swing had begun. Mr. Hyde was gone. For now, I would spend the next week being the charming Dr. Jekyll, wining and dining all the employees. With the potential exposure of my over billing by such a colossal mistake, I needed the protection of my employees. Maybe it was not too late.

The powers that be were ready to deal with me. Poachers would come and remove this gorilla from his steel jungle, kicking and screaming. Motivated by their own fears, good conscience and I now accept, the will of God, Don Myers and one of my nurses, Dianne Trissler, had turned me into the feds.

As I've Learned

I'm convinced that an honest mistake is so often what trips up dishonesty. We're so sure how clever we are but the truth always comes out. I just didn't know it yet. My old rodeo was coming to an end. I was about to find out the bronc rider I egotistically imagined myself to be was really just a rodeo clown. The wheels of justice that would grind me down had started turning my direction right there, in September, 2000.

Egomania is a lot scarier than any possible bird flu pandemic. Egomania is an American epidemic and spreading fast. It's contagious. Most people deny a problem with ego. I sure did. Besides, I never thought of myself as being egotistical, I figured I really was great.

Denial causes more chaos than a tornado in all areas of our lives. For me, I was denying that my ego was driving me to focus on wealth and all the trappings of success, with no moral measures. I was busy denying that greed, pride and arrogance were driving me to live a life far from the moral teachings of my childhood and this denial caused ego to rampage through my life like a tornado. My behavior was typical of the monster I was becoming. When we let our ego and our fears take control of our lives, we truly become monsters and the devil's own.

Chapter 5

Twilight: FBI Raid

On March 26, 2001, three dozen FBI, OIG and ATF agents blasted their way into my office armed with AK-47s and held me at gunpoint. As the result of a long FBI investigation, I was later charged with healthcare fraud.

I should have seen it coming, and maybe I did, somewhere in a drug-induced haze. Years before, I'd begun trading one addiction for another, going from cocaine to Klonopin, among an impressive list of others. Sure, the drugs had probably clouded my judgment but my problems started long before I began taking the pills. My life had been out of control for a very long time and I'd ignored all the warning signs from my wife, from my parents and siblings, from my friends. I thought I could handle anything that came along, cheat the Medicare system with over billings, double billings and keep on dancing.

I thought I was on top of the world. I could have anything, be anything, control everything.

Only I couldn't and I hadn't been in control for years, as I soon learned, it would take five more years to figure that out. The process wasn't going to be easy. Sometimes, as the lies weighed me down, I toyed with the idea of getting caught. I wouldn't have to pretend anymore. On that day in March 2001, I wasn't thinking too clearly. I was losing everything I thought mattered to me and my life was spinning out of control. Then I realized I had just wanted to walk away because I was growing afraid.

My feelings were chaotic; doubt, sorrow, anger, anxiety, resentment and oddly enough, peace took turns rushing through me. While having any degree of peace may sound strange, it was a relief to finally get caught. The tension of waiting for something bad to happen was over, even though I knew I'd committed a crime for which there was a penalty.

Like most failed criminals, I had run what I had thought was the perfect operation. My company furnished durable medical equipment and supplies for Medicare participants, all fully covered under Medicare and perfectly legal. But my operations were far from legal. There was a huge gap between my inventory and sales reported, compared to my actual sales and merchandise delivery; but I convinced myself that as long as the cash flow kept up and Medicare didn't check it's billings too closely, I was doing fine. Better than fine since I had an income in six figures and the ability to manufacture more revenue by manipulating the billing system. Was it honest?

Obviously not. Did I care? Absolutely not. The money came so easily that the good life seemed a slam-dunk until the FBI showed up in my office.

The entire morning of the raid still seems like watching a movie to me. For some time, I'd known someone must have been onto my illegal operations. I could sense I was being watched, because the FBI doesn't always hide it's surveillance, almost as if the feds want their prey to be aware of and fear being followed. I wasn't alone in this feeling. My employees could sense this presence too.

The same faces seemed to crop up everywhere, strangers in crowds, in stores and restaurants but those same faces became all too familiar. During phone calls, echoes of voices and noises that didn't originate at either end of the phone line invaded our calls. In my rearview mirror I'd see the same car (or cars) continually popping up. Was I being followed? They followed me way too close for their presence to be a coincidence. For someone used to playing head games, I was now on the receiving end. We had incidental visits from "companies" in regards to the building we were leasing. These company representatives asked far too many questions about our day-to-day operations of the company and more specifically, about me.

My staff finally had enough the day they had seen "that woman," again. She was one of those faces that kept popping up when they went out to lunch or to shop. This time, she was spotted at The Gap, the popular national clothing chain, while they shopped during lunch. "That woman," as it turned out, was to be Tiffany Black, the lead federal agent on my case.

Looking back on the month preceding the raid, it was as if a huge fog had blanketed my life and my common sense. Logic told me that I knew I'd be caught, that it was only a matter of time. Sadly, right up to the minute the raid began, a part of me was still in denial. Even before the raid began that morning, I felt a sense of doom. I was very sad and had that dreamlike feeling of moving through quicksand. I sensed something bad was about to happen. I was tense and volatile, flying into rages over minor matters. The difference now was I couldn't deny I was drifting out of control. My rages would do no good for me now. Anything and everything would set me off. Coupled with the fact that by nature I'm a hothead, my staff fed off my tension and tried to stay clear of me while I was in such a foul mood.

The people who worked for me were scared of me. They saw me as a monster, literally and by then, I was. Fueled by drugs, alcohol and a fast-living, fast-track lifestyle, I was impossible to live with at home or at work. I began as a free-spending, fast-money guy and ended up as a combination of Dr. Jekyll and Mr. Hyde. The problem was, most days, Mr. Hyde was the only one who showed up at work. My employees never knew if they would be working for Jekyll or Hyde on any given day.

Nevertheless, on the morning of the raid, my already high anxiety level was off the charts. More reason for me to eat Klonopin for breakfast. I remember taking more than usual that morning. In sober minutes, I began to sense I might get caught sooner or later. The Klonopin helped tone down my constant anxiety over reality. When the time did come, the one thing I wanted to avoid was having my wife and baby girl witness what happened. In the weeks before the raid, I'd kept playing in my mind different scenarios of getting caught and where. At church? At lunch? At the airport? At my parents' home? At my in-laws' home? Strangely, I didn't envision the raid occurring at the most obvious place, my office.

Several of my priorities went through my mind: the money I'd made dishonestly and how I'd miss the trappings of success it bought, the wasted years, my pregnant wife at home with our first baby, Mica, what my family would think, how long I'd go to prison, who ratted me out and I thought, how God would view me getting caught. I had, instead, made a deal of sorts with the devil. After all, I was a Christian! Looking back and seeing men just like I was, it's easy for me to see now how I scared others away from religion. They must have thought, "If Rodd's an example of what it means to be a Christian, I want nothing to do with it!" That's how most, if not everyone, saw me then. One of my employees once said, "Mr. Brown, you're the kind of Christian that takes change out of the offering basket, aren't you?" I didn't do that, although I certainly cheated many people out of huge sums but I sure fit the profile of those who would stoop to such pettiness. I epitomized the lost lamb whose relationship with God was meaningless, reduced to plastering the little fish logo on my bumper sticker or having a cross printed on business cards.

When I first began writing this book, I seriously

considered entitling it: Get Out Of My Way For God's Sakes!

Spring, 2001

As for getting caught and having to own up to my crime, I'd envisioned an FBI agent coming up to me, politely tapping me on the shoulder and advising me of my rights. I had no idea that the raid would be so large, with so many federal agents and so many guns! Reality slapped me down at 9:01 that March morning, when I discovered I'd totally underrated the intensity of the feds and their ability to completely set my circus down.

When the initial squad, decked in bulletproof armor from head to toe, entered the building screaming and shouting, I had a serious out-of body-experience. My staff and I stood open-mouthed at the chaos erupting around us while the agents screamed at us.

"Who's Rodd Brown?"
"Who's Rodd Brown?"
"Who's Rodd Brown?"

They were shouting for someone to identify me, waving AK-47s and throwing my terrified employees, one of whom was my Uncle Mark (who had began working for me one year earlier) from their chairs to the floor. Dogs were barking. Employees were crying. Feds were yelling and I was being dragged by two agents down the hall into my office, where for a very long time agents surrounded me with their assault weapons aimed at me, just inches away from my head. I remember wondering what the hell was going on.

Once I was cornered at my desk, they said not a word to me for the first thirty minutes. They just kept their rifles pointed inches from my head as if I were a violent serial killer about to make my escape, while other agents throughout the building secured the employees and the rest of the building. I had entered the twilight zone, without Rod Serling to cheerfully announce that a brief change was about to take place. Briefly, I wondered whether this was actually happening or whether this whole experience was a particularly vivid nightmare and any moment I'd wake up safe in my bed at home.

While the agents were still holding me at gunpoint, the feds began releasing my employees, one by one. They had all agreed to meet across the street at a Bennigan's restaurant. Finally, the armed men were given instructions by the agent in charge, Tiffany, to "pull back." I was released, not free but at least not at gunpoint anymore.

As the raid went on, I began to wonder whether I was losing my mind. My thoughts were so jumbled I'm sure I was not thinking rationally. The only clear image that kept rolling through my mind was the certainty that I'd leave my office that day in handcuffs and I'd be gone for a very long time. I wondered fleetingly what my wife would say and do; then began going down a list of people who would be hurt by the terrible choices I'd made. Mom, Dad, Scott, Todd and their families came right after my wife Cari and my infant daughter. My unborn child. Somehow, God didn't stay on my list once I was caught. He was useful to protect me and He had let me down. I had no idea it would be five years before I finally realized how much

I'd hurt the loving, forgiving, God and allow Him to touch my heart!

The missing part about that morning was that during all the years I was committing fraud, cheating others, I lived with the firm conviction, which I conveniently ignored, that my life "belonged to God." I recalled handing out communion at church, as a sign for others to look toward our Savior for the pattern by which we should be living. I had known I was doing the wrong thing. Dishonesty went against every moral principle I'd ever been taught but I was doing nothing about it. I believed in Jesus Christ as my Savior but was too egotistical to act on that faith. I was lukewarm in the way I observed my faith. I spent twenty years knowing that God had called my life to His purpose and I ran from Him as fast and as far as I could during all that time. The whole country was in a horrible tailspin. A few months later, the 9/11 tragedy struck, then the Enron scandal hit. I vividly remember calling my attorney, Joel Bernstein and discussing my case with him. Joel was an incredibly well-spoken attorney who had the gift of sheer genius gab. He could spin a normal sentence into a eulogy of sorts. Nevertheless, on the phone that day I was very inquisitive and I poured out a barrage of questions, as usual.

"Have you heard from the feds? Am I going to prison? What have they found? Are they looking at anyone else? How much longer?"

My increasing anxiety about not knowing my fate gave me a burden of crippling fear. I vividly remember him saying to me on the phone that day, "Rodd, there's planes falling out of the sky in New York City and they're having an energy crisis in Houston. Your case will go unnoticed."

Cautiously, I believed him. I wanted to believe him but given all I had done, it was hard to imagine that my case would go unnoticed.

With the fed's seizure of my business, bank accounts and assets, my show of success had called the curtain down. It took just a few short days for my wife and I to become officially dead broke. Having no money makes for a very difficult marriage in and of itself. I had no idea that day that the indictments wouldn't be handed down for another three years and our financial woes had only begun. We were soon on Food Stamps and WIC (Women, Infants and Children), a program for those in poverty to receive dairy products through the government. I had put my family on welfare!

Mind you, Cari had nothing to do with the criminal life I lived, absolutely nothing. Nothing, except for trusting in me when we got married. She was a very beautiful woman with a loving heart and was dealt a bad hand by a living monster. She did the very best she could, given the fact I had wanted her enough, at first, to care for nothing else. Nothing, in other words, except that I wanted to have her, no matter how much I could hurt her.

Like the good woman she was, Cari waited in lines at the grocery stores to pay with Food Stamps and WIC. She sat through long, hot hours at the welfare office to learn of any programs that would relieve our financial mess.

Cari Grimes could have married almost any man

she wanted, yet she chose me. My mistakes were huge; trying to chain her to a marriage with me was much bigger than a mistake. It was a sin, it was a rejection of what marriage really means.

It's fair to wonder and seriously contemplate, were we Dr. and Mrs. Jekyll or Mr. and Mrs. Hyde?

Cari grew weary of the life I presented and justifiably filed for divorce. When the divorce was final and it was time for me to pay child support, I dangled what money I had over her head, accusing her that she would spend the money on herself. It was a horrible thing to do to her and the kids but it was part of Rodd, the monster. I would lie, tell her the payment had been made, knowing full well it hadn't. I blamed the Child Support Division for mishandling the money!

As I've learned.

Shutting God out from your life is a very lonely way to live. At some level, you know you've been called to follow Him and to do nothing about it leaves a black emptiness inside. When I did speak of Christ, anyone who heard my voice laughed and thought, "What a hypocrite!" and for good reason. I was like the Pharisee who spoke of God with his mouth but his heart was far from God.

In truth, most of all the day of my fall, I was looking for someone to blame, anyone but myself. God hadn't fixed things for me. He'd let me get caught. I was angry with God and I felt betrayed by Him for what was happening. For so long I had played the "if only" game with God.

Dear God, if only . . . .
If only you get me the new house . . . .
If only you get me more money . . . .
If only my wife and I have more sex . . . .
If only you get me through this mess . . . .
If only my wife doesn't learn of
my indiscretions . . . .

Naturally, I never asked for, "If only you put me through three drug rehabs, three marriages, federal prison, halfway house, being homeless, then I would surrender my life to you," but that's exactly what happened. So much for us playing the "If only" game!

In anger, I asked where was the love of God when deadly assault rifles were pointed inches from my head, when I was booked for healthcare fraud, when my business was in ruin? Where was all that greatness that God promises is our birthright through his love? And where was God when the large, metal door slammed shut, dooming me to serve in FCI Ft. Worth, a low secured facility, to live the next year with two-thousand inmates whose crimes ranged from my white-collar crime to murder?

Where is God when the pain is severe? When we really hurt and are truly suffering? God is actually closer than we think. God was right there but I wasn't aware of that yet. I still had a lot to learn about His love and how it could transform my life.

Friends, it's during our struggles that God finally has an opportunity to remind us how much He loves us and is willing to forgive at all costs.

There are times in our lives when things don't nearly work out the way we want them to or the way we think they will or should. Sometimes we don't even see it coming. In my case, it should have been very obvious. We are blind-sided with this incredible situation, this enormous amount of pain that buckles our knees and leaves us all but speechless and then we are left feeling desperate and helpless.

As I have learned through my journey, that's life. We are left wondering how and why God can let these things happen to us. How can God not intervene but instead just stand back and watch us suffer. As I have learned, God takes men into deep waters not to drown them but rather to cleanse them.

I could have easily listened to God the day of the raid. I chose to ignore Him. I learned the hard way there are two choices at rock bottom. One, let it be the bottom and start climbing back up. Two, ignore the pain and opportunity and find out there's more where that came from.

Believe me when I say this, if I can witness to others, if God can change my heart, if I can give my life completely and without reserve to God, then so can you. There was not a name or reputation worse than mine by the time my business crumbled and I went to prison. The name "Rodd Brown" was simply detested by many.

The contradiction for me is seeing God work through me, to address the problems that were my downfall. Many times my message is to never do it the "Rodd Brown" way.

Funny, Scott now jokes that I taught Todd and

nobody taught me! It's terribly refreshing to look back at struggle and laugh about it.

Nevertheless, the old Rodd Brown way was the way to ruin. Today, through God's grace and gifts, I am able to share my pain, cry with grown men whose wives have left, speak to families whose kids have run away from home, listen to businessmen speak about their financial problems and offer the only thing I really know at this point, God's amazing grace and unconditional love. The more honest I can be about my life, the more forgiveness I experience.

Being able to learn and love through trials is very difficult but it can be done. In fact, we must do it: if we intend to change for the better! I've done it and you can too. God has big plans for all of us. As a pastor once said, "If you've only been saved thirty seconds, you have a story that can help someone." For me, as a recovering addict, my salvation is only a day old, one day at a time.

Chapter 6

Jigsaw Man: The Addict

One thing I learn in looking back at my life is just how many pieces of life I was holding in my hands. Perhaps not a million little pieces but there were plenty, nonetheless. In most ways, I was just a jigsaw puzzle. But I wasn't the only one. From the people I lied to in business, those I was to meet in prison and many of the people who gladly took my money while condemning the way I made it; I look back and also see so many of us fit together in temporary schemes of deceit.

I was a super freak on a super freak-out! My crazy life as a highly successful executive in public and a man totally out of control in private was fueled by my chemical addictions. Still, make no mistake about blaming addictions for a problem; I used drugs just the same way I used people, false billing forms and my family. I was becoming just shreds and shards of cardboard, held together by glue and greed, just a human jigsaw puzzle with more pieces missing every day; and when the pieces refused to fit, I just pushed harder and cut more edges from my mind.

As I said earlier, the FBI's raid should not have come as a surprise and in reality, it didn't but one of the side effects of chemical dependency is impaired judgment and a dampening effect on moral judgment. No excuses. I chose to do what I did. In inner turmoil over the feds' shutdown of my business, outstanding checks that bounced, the loss of home and family, I faced a struggle with the grim future ahead by entering rehab. I did not do it with the desire to change but to put some temporary distance between my troubles and myself and to get more favorable treatment by the judge at sentencing. My high-priced lawyer was reassuring at first but the legal bills mounted with no clear resolution of my problems in sight. I was angry, hostile and still dependent on Klonopin, feeling the world was against me. Because I am convinced we are headed for a world of addiction, unless we speak up and begin to act, I want to write from my heart about what I feel I've come to understand about the jigsaw of addictive excuses.

Pressure is constantly building every day in every part of our lives. The state of the world, terror and the gruesome acts we read about daily, weigh our hearts down with sorrow. It's no wonder we seek to escape. Alcohol and drugs have been part of society for as long and as far back as you want to look.

Addiction to drugs and alcohol is nothing new, it's existed for centuries. But the changing scene in America starting in the 1960s and flowering through the first part of the 1970s began a new age of permissiveness. The erstwhile Harvard professor, Dr. Timothy Leary (as I mentioned earlier) epitomized the counter-culture of that age with his advice to, "Turn on. Tune in. Drop out." He touted the psychedelic drug LSD. Marijuana came into popular use and young people followed Leary's advice by the thousands. It was an era of protest against authority in any form, fueled by the unpopular war in Vietnam. "Peace" and "Love" became watchwords and political and social protests were considered hip. The Age of Aquarius became the Age of Disillusionment and "Never trust anyone over thirty!" became it's slogan.

Children rebelled against everything their parents stood for. Stability, hard work, family-centered values, all went by the wayside as the youth of America pursued happiness without taking responsibility for their actions. The sixties rolled into the seventies and when the Watergate scandal erupted in 1974, the counter-culture generation pointed to a loss of faith in government, order and justice.

Once the genie is out of the bottle, it's not possible to put it back in and drug use continued to be the "in" thing to do. For my parents, alcohol had been the drug of choice but now there was a whole smorgasbord of new and interesting substances to experiment with. As the eighties began, the laid-back attitudes of the sixties and seventies evolved into what many sociologists called the "Me" generation. Success was the most important thing and the mellowing effects of the psychedelic drugs were traded for the mind-blowing highs of cocaine. Success was measured in who made the biggest killing on Wall Street, who drove the latest Beamer or Mercedes, who got the fastest and biggest promotions. Cocaine became the "can-do" drug because it made it's users feel they could do anything. It gave them the heady rush of speed, of feeling on top of the world. Even the tightening of drug control laws did little to slow down it's usage among the affluent. The fact that coke came with a high price tag made it a symbol of success among many of us young, well-to-do professionals.

With the range of substances available, legal and illegal, it's easy to see how alcohol could seem tame by comparison, although drinking often became the first gateway into experimentation with other drugs. Social drinking had been acceptable for generations. The "Me" generation just took it a step further. By the time I reached college, the laws were getting far more stringent against drug use; but the supply was still there, if one knew the right sources and I always could find the right source. I didn't need to look any further than my own college classmates.

Most of us, not all, but I would guess the high percentage of the population, have at some time or another sought to escape from problems and pressures and the high induced by alcohol or drugs is a temporary escape. It's no longer just tobacco and alcohol that are available to us but a variety of synthesized concoctions. As if alcohol and tobacco don't do enough damage! As world conditions worsen, our need to find greater escapes increase and thus, we as a society find ourselves in a spiral of hell; addictions feeding off world conditions and world conditions feeding off our addictions. Let me stress here that all these rationales for escape are just that-rationales, not reasons.

USA Today published an article recently stating that one in every five Americans is an addict. Addiction is an epidemic, even as our types of addictions continue to multiply. An addict is defined as somebody who is "physiologically or mentally dependent on a drug liable to have damaging physiological or psychological effects." An addict is also defined as an enthusiast, somebody who is devoted to something. Sure I was enthusiastic in my desires and I gave myself wholeheartedly to achieving my objectives. I developed a dependency on all the wrong things through my misguided enthusiasm. My addictive personality is part of what brought me down.

There is a misconception that in order to be sociable, we need to have a certain image and the accoutrements of alcohol and drugs help to build that image. Of course, I was the center of attention throughout most of the parties; it was part of the entire image. There are just some guys who are the life of the party.

I never had a problem with cigarettes and if you took away alcohol, drugs, money and sex I really didn't have any addictions! I mean, everyone drinks, does drugs and wants more money and more sex, right? Wrong! That's part of the madness, thinking that everyone has the same problems. Along the way, I kept telling myself the ultimate Addict's Lie, "I can quit anytime I want to. I don't have a problem with substance abuse."

As for the "I can quit anytime" theory, it's absolutely true. And absolutely misleading. The problem is in the ambiguity in the word "anytime." This is the cliché, a denial phrase for anyone who smokes, drinks or knows he has a problem but doesn't want to admit it. We use that word to coach us through more time. We justify the "anytime" phrase because as we are saying it, we really haven't hit rock bottom yet and we are still trying to convince ourselves that our addictions are helping us to "relax" to avoid that bottom. The problem is that the bottom will come and we will either die or recover. "I can quit anytime" is our own little way of admitting to ourselves that we don't have a terminal problem today. Ironically, you can say this phrase and not two sentences later, judge exactly what everyone else's problems are; their addictions, their fears and their issues. Perhaps the folks who began marketing Happy Hour would like to copyright the phrase, "I can quit anytime!" It would certainly boost revenues.

There is never enough to satiate a soul that has a hole in it. Everything given to it or placed in its care, trickles out the bottom. An addiction works no differently than a radiator that has overheated. It never allows a car to cool itself and perform as it was intended. At worst, the engine will completely overheat, break down and perhaps blow up. What we don't realize is that God's holy spirit is the plug to this hole in our soul, giving us the ability to hold life in our hearts, take in love and be content in life. If we don't reject His love to fill the hole, the void in our souls, then we absolutely will have the opportunity to perform as humans to our greatest abilities and to use the gifts granted to us by our creator as they were intended. We can become the high performance machines we were intended to be under God's plan.

For all those lost years, I always wanted to believe there were problems much larger in scale and scope than mine. Men and women all over the world were addicted to drugs, alcohol, money and sex, far worse than I was. And of course, yes, there are those that were worse. But as long as we see our problems as incidental or minimal we will never get well or free. Never! For some reason we seem to minimize our own folly through the hardships, addictions and struggles of others, don't we? Of course we do! But, the sad reality is that we are stuck in our own world of perceptions. No matter what, no one else is living our lives, so we can never truly understand what, "walking in another man's shoes," is all about.

It doesn't matter if you are about to lose a Donald Trump-like fortune, or the beaten travel trailer you live in, as you try to rebuild your life. It's your world you live in and not your things. They are your problems and no one can or should try to minimize them by ignoring them.

So I was in denial concerning my drug and alcohol addiction, convincing everyone that my addiction was small in scale in comparison to that of others; but they were still addictions and they still led to the crashing down of my world. When that happened, there was no denying their existence or importance anymore.

When you are sitting in a chair with six FBI agents on each side of you and assault rifles aimed at you, reality takes a new direction. Sure, I still tried to deny my wrongdoings and I certainly didn't think that my addictions were anything that had to do with my present quandary. In fact, as I left that day with the feds, I found myself needing to unwind. After all, who wouldn't need a drink or a fix after a day like that? We all need releases and that is the theme I played in my head, over and over, "This is just a little something I deserve to release a bit of stress. It's normal and healthy and I will die without it."

The reality is that my addictions were killing me! They were killing me and killing my family. Drugs and alcohol, which is where it all began for me, are the ideal products for Satan, the ultimate merchandise. No sales talk necessary. The client will crawl through a sewer and beg to buy. We all know, or have been around an addict, haven't we?

Fall, 2001

My addiction to Klonopin, a very potent Benzodiazepine that affects the nervous system (normal dosage is .5-2 milligrams per day and I was taking 6-10 milligrams), was simply profound. I had grown to the point of beyond control. Literally, my thoughts, emotions, feelings, love and devotion had all been surrendered to the care of those little pills. For the first time in ten years, I had completely run out of my pills. In spite of everything going on, I managed to forget having my prescription refilled. Of all things, I forgot my prescription. This was the most unforgivable act I could have done to myself at the time.

I had just divorced for a second time, while my

second daughter was being born. On top of the federal raid, I had applied for bankruptcy, was being forced to repay the District Attorney's Office $1400 per month remuneration, was waiting for food stamps and WIC to approve me and had lost almost every possession I had. My BMW had been repossessed a few days earlier and I was the center of an IRS investigation. I would have preferred someone to set me on fire rather than to forget my prescription of Klonopin.

I was a nervous wreck. I was living alone at 1321 Dartmouth in Denton. I bought this house a few months after college graduation. The house had been a symbol of my rising star status. Now it was a refuge, where I had run aground after losing my upscale home in Southlake.

My mind was racing. Gloom weighed heavily in my thoughts. My anxiety was piercing. My palms began sweating, as did my forehead and most of my body and there was this horrible taste in my mouth that, for some reason, reminded me of battery acid. I have no idea why my mind chose battery acid but it did and I couldn't shake the taste. I had never been around battery acid in my life. That night, my mind actually believed my mouth tasted like battery acid!

Desperate and in a frenzy, I grabbed the phone and quickly punched in 1411. Without even giving the operator a chance to greet me, I cut her off and demanded the number of Albertson's pharmacy in Denton. She went through the series of questions to confirm my request as she began the search, following every protocol in the book. While I could rationalize this as an exercise in some training room, there was no comprehension, the woman was simply trying to kill me. I wanted my Klonopin.

"Ma'am do you have to be dumb your whole life?" I demanded, pacing the floor and seriously feeling like harming myself or something or someone else. It was a horrible feeling. Next I tried sarcasm. "I mean, I know you only make the minimum wage but, hurry! Do something good for the first time in your life!"

Of course, she requested that I calm down, lower my voice and listen to reason but I was beyond reason and rage welled up in me like a fire. With each question she asked, I became more belittling and contemptuous of her. Every time she requested I lower my voice, I screamed louder that I wasn't screaming. All I could think of was how I could get my hands on just one of those little yellow pills. I was out of control and abusing someone through a telephone line. All I wanted was my fix and all she wanted was someone to give her the chance to do her job. She was probably very good at it. Obviously, in hindsight, my rage prevented either of these things from happening at the moment and she asked if I would like to speak with a supervisor.

How incompetent could a person be? All I was asking for was a number to a common pharmacy in my hometown. Of course, she had to be kidding. So I asked her, "Are you kidding me?"

Her reply echoed in my head, "No sir. No sir. No sir . . ." She wasn't kidding and if I was anywhere near her I probably would have been beaten her to a pulp. She was polite and attempting to be helpful and all

I heard was a condescending, uncooperative woman who was refusing to help me. So we spent the next twenty minutes, at least, going back and forth with me demanding her name and her telling me that is was against policy for her to give it to me; then offering to pass me to a supervisor. This circle of hell had me almost ripping my own head off.

Eventually she transferred me to a supervisor in her nice polite way. Stunned, I sat there screaming into the phone as it went through its series of beeps while transferring, as the polite but unhelpful operator had warned me it would. The supervisor had little more to offer. When he finally said that my only choice was to be nice or be cut off and start over, I knew I had to somehow regain control.

Needless to say, I punched in the numbers and could not believe what I heard. "Thank you for calling Albertson's, your good neighbor pharmacy and food store. For instructions in English, please press one . . . ."

"You have got to be kidding me!" I screamed. Every reaction I had was a textbook case of symptoms and actions of an addict. My body needed this drug and I would not stop until I got it.

I wanted desperately to throw the phone through the wall! I took a breath, then a series of deeper ones. I checked my watch and realized it was a few minutes past midnight. For two hours I had been trying to get my prescription filled. My thoughts were skewed, racing and irrational. Physically, I trembled and sweat dripped over my entire body. Sweat rings had formed in both armpits, around my neck, in the small of my back and across my chest. I couldn't believe I was actually going through this. I was an absolute wreck!

Through my frenzy, I managed to hang the phone up. Pacing and angry, I punched the redial button. "Thank you for calling . . ."

"One!" "One!" "One!" I yelled, "One!" as I punched the button for English. I peeked through the front window again, for whatever reason. I hoped no one could hear me and call the police to investigate. Another human at this point would be catastrophic. I could hardly put a sentence together, much less be face-to-face with someone! Suddenly another recording came on. "Thank you for calling the Albertson's Pharmacy, located at 1210 West University Drive in Denton."

Screaming for the operator, I am sure my neighbors thought I was being murdered. I punched the zero button for the store operator at least a dozen times! I couldn't handle more recordings. A moment later I thought my luck had changed when I heard,

"Thank you for calling . . ."

"Pharmacy please."

"I do apologize, sir, they closed at midnight."

"You bitch!" I screamed.

It was no more than five minutes after midnight and I had failed to find a way to get my fix. My anger had clouded me so that I was unable to get what I needed out of the situation. Granted, I was trying to fulfill my drug addiction but this is not entirely different than many other addictions we are faced with daily. Had I taken a breath with the first operator and simply calmed myself down, instead of assuming that everyone was stupid and incompetent (except me), I would have filled my prescription an hour earlier. Instead, I was the one who was incompetent, unable to do the simplest of tasks without consuming hours of energy, filled with hatred toward people who were only trying to help.

Three weeks later and with the help of an exhausted family, I checked myself into New Life Rehabilitation Center in Phoenix, Arizona, where I spent the most grueling and agonizing five weeks of my life in withdrawal, hallucinations, chills, body sweats, mood swings, irrational thoughts and overwhelming irritability. I spent the next year bouncing sporadically through outpatient programs and at least half a dozen psychiatrists before realizing the insanity to my recovery. As I have learned and share with many today, if your heart's not in the recovery and there is no God, you will never truly understand the depth or your personal hell; or even worse, you will never recover, never!

Unquestionably, entering a drug rehab program is filled with shame and fear. The day I walked through the doors for my first day of drug rehab, my heart was beating so hard I thought it would burst out of my chest. I thought I was going to have a heart attack. I wasn't there by my own design and this only made matters worse. I was examined and my belongings searched. At the very least, the staff would force the toxins out of my body. If they were truly successful, they would force the toxic thoughts out of my brain, which had allowed me to seek solace in drugs and alcohol.

It took what seemed like forever, as my body shook and trembled.

Chuck, the most brilliant rehab counselor in the world, later explained that taking me off that much Klonopin "cold-turkey" was equivalent to driving a car for ten years at 100 mph, then suddenly hitting a tree. This is what addiction does. I hit the tree and I hit it hard.

As I've learned.

Addiction is much bigger than just your own life. It is a problem for an entire community and even for the world. As your addictions get fed, you take from others instead of offering love and that feeds their fears and leads more into the epidemic of addiction. We must start small, with ourselves. I truly believe that we can effect this change, one person at a time. This is all we have. It starts with faith in God and knowing that He will help us overcome what we fear.

I remember sitting in my cell and just thinking back on everything. Just one big mess. There were carcasses and feelings scattered throughout the United States and at the time I was completely oblivious to it. Others would say I had a problem and I always gave excuses. Always. The problem with a rational man is he can rationalize away his emotions or his misgivings. This only leads to bigger fears and a matrix of unprocessed emotions that can be overwhelming unless you soothe them with the numbing effects of alcohol or drugs. We don't like the lives we have created and we want to escape.

Addiction is a prison in itself. To feel the

emptiness, the solitude and the pain of addiction puts steel bars around the soul. You believe that nothing else matters. Like all addicts, I told myself I could stop at anytime. That's one comfort an addict uses to keep right on with his habit. I have never talked to anyone who's recovered from addiction who wishes to be back in the grip of drugs.

It's funny but addiction was also a lot like my first job after college selling used cars. There are no really good stories about that life. In selling used cars, we all spoke of the things we were going to do, the successes we would have and the life we all wanted and wished for. The car lot was simply a holding tank of dreams interrupted. There were very good men on that car lot but men who never could get their feet underneath them. Like prison, we spoke of better days or great days gone by. It's the same with addiction and recovery. There aren't great stories shared during the midst of it. I have never heard someone say, "Man, I wish I was still an addict." Rather, we pray for those still suffering. Addiction is the result of, among many other things, the loss of hope or dignity. When we feel there is no other way to go, we turn to substances that give us the feeling, just for a moment, that we are in control.

Addiction numbed the pain of knowing how much my family suffered for the love they had for me and how much their loyalty cost them. It's sure okay to love one who is addicted but sometimes loving means the tough love a parent must have for a child, confronting him with his actions. That gives hope to both the addict and those who love him. In the months that followed that raid on my office, I learned that God can deliver anyone. He delivered me from the grip of despair, from the sin I'd committed and from a life that was filled with pain.

My dear friends, drug misuse is not a disease, it is a decision; like the decision to step out in front of a moving car. You would call that not a disease but an error of judgment. Drugs are simply reality's escape from God.

Why are we addicted? It's often very simple. We haven't come to terms with who we are. We drink or take drugs to escape reality; but what are we really escaping? Ourselves! We don't want to see ourselves as we have been made, or play the deck we have been dealt, so we begin by temporarily escaping with drugs, alcohol, money, sex. I remember when it all started with my use of alcohol in high school. From there it went to drugs, then sex, then money and it became this vicious cycle that was literally out of control and very dangerous. In my first rehab, a counselor told me I was doing enough drugs to have literally "killed the normal man!" At some point, addiction goes from a very generic drink or drug to a life completely addicted to chaos.

Since leaving prison, I am required to attend counseling every Thursday with Dr. Henry. I was very familiar with Dr. Henry, since I was ordered into counseling as part of my pre-trial requirements. The relationship between me and Dr. Henry is one of the many I couldn't enjoy before going to prison, because I was not ready to receive. Now I am and I seriously look forward to Thursday mornings because I not only enjoy but also appreciate his teachings. His lessons didn't change, I did. Please note that you don't need to be a dysfunctional addict, living on the streets and prostituting yourself for your next fix. Most addicts are highly functional and professional and can create the illusion that there is nothing wrong in their lives. I was this type of addict.

Dr. Henry began explaining, through proven theory, the power of addiction. He said that he was working in a methadone clinic treating heroin addicts and he remembered one man in particular who had gone through the treatment center after being in prison for ten years. This particular addict was from upstate New York and he would be leaving Texas to return to New York, after having kicked heroin for ten years.

He boarded the train for his commute home and immediately began getting nauseated. As the train got closer and closer to New York and the addict's former neighborhood, he was becoming noticeably sicker and sicker. He began having physical pains in his stomach. He began sweating. As the train arrived in his hometown and he could literally see the streets where he once dealt and used heroin, he literally began throwing up! After ten years without heroin and being locked up in a prison, the power of addiction had caused him to puke all over the train! Ten years of sobriety and just entering the streets and neighborhoods of where it all began made this man physically sick! Ten years!

For the sake of your friends and family, at least until you learn to love yourself again, give up your addictions for them! I remember in my first rehab hearing the serenity prayer and it says, " . . . and we pray for those still suffering." I remember sitting in that rehab unit in Arizona after the FBI raid, being completely broke to the point of needing food stamps, of realizing that my wife had learned of my infidelity and knowing there was still prison time to serve. I wondered if I would ever be at a place in life, safe and well enough to pray for those still suffering. My wondering has been answered. I am now in a place safe enough to pray for those still suffering. It's in the amazing grace of God, no doubt about it!

Incredibly, the easier life is the graceful life. We can work so hard at being able to fit into other people's expectations, we miss the simple pleasures. In the end, honesty is always a lot easier to remember than the string of lies we have to work too hard to remember.

Chapter 7
Worn Out: Sentenced

By the end of 2003, I was simply exhausted. In those dark days following my divorce, when I racked up multiple civil lawsuits, endless depositions, trips back and forth to Houston to see my attorney, my bankruptcy, repossessions, foreclosures, pending indictments, tens of thousands of dollars in hot checks and I had lost most of my friends and family, I found refuge (again!) with my last, most loyal friend-Klonopin, even after detox and rehab. Addictions, you see, are friends to the very end.

Naturally, I managed to shop around for physicians to prescribe amounts much larger than anyone should use. I began taking an extraordinary amount of Klonopin. My words began to slur, almost as if I had a speech impediment. I blamed the doctors. I blamed stress. I stared in mirrors, shocked at my own face.

My inner conflict was more than I could stand. I drank too much booze and managed to up my intake of Klonopin. Often, I'd begin drinking during the morning and continue throughout the day, until Cari and I would be engaged in a screaming match by nightfall. All of it was my fault. Nevertheless, I fought each time for an immediate victory. My kingdom came down to these last four walls. The fights were ridiculous, about the most trivial matters but they were more than enough to fuel the monster inside me. We'd argue about what we were having for dinner, the way she dressed, how we were rearing the children. We'd fight about money or the lack thereof in our case. Anything was fair game for a fight in my head and sadly, Cari could only fight back. No longer able to leave Cari alone during the day, I could see she was shocked at just how volatile I was. If she worried what I was capable of doing to her or even to the children, I can understand it now, barely. When we begin to heal, our shame can drag us back to hide from our responsibility.

The worst part of those days was that, somewhere in my twisted reactions, I knew better than to act this way. I was certainly not raised to behave toward my family in such a manner. My life growing up was simply magical and there was a sense of the boy in me, somewhere, even during those dark days. Now, instead of taking responsibility, I desperately wanted to return to those innocent days of magic. But I was incapable of finding meaning in my own life and just wanted to hide behind my image of past innocence. Thank God I couldn't hide any more.

Getting back to a normal life seemed too difficult, since I told myself I couldn't even find a starting point. I see now I was making it too complicated.

There was no one who really wanted anything to do with me, which made me even angrier. My parents and brothers had all retreated, simply avoiding me at all costs. They did their best to love me from a distance and that was very hard for them because we had always been a warm, close loving family. They all have an amazing family love and huge hearts and it was difficult for them not to love me as they wanted. They still loved me, just not as much as they wanted to.

Miracles, as I've learned, aren't complicated. Miracle aren't always lighting bolts or walking on water but rather being able to pick your kids up and take them to McDonald's and play, carefree. Laugh with your siblings. Call your dad on the phone and tell jokes. Love your mother with all your heart and soul as she has done you. These, friends, are miracles that I've been given and there is nothing better.

None of this was going to awaken in me for several more years and I would keep learning the hard way. Strangely, through all of this chaos, I was living a life convinced that I really knew what God wanted from me and I ran like hell in the other direction. I was scared of giving up the 'good life'. Yes, the good life. The same living that nearly cost me my life!

It should be needless to say but my anger and addictions were both out of control. Throughout the town where I grew up, dozens of people believed I'd either kill myself or someone else would do the job. Both were very possible.

My life was simply a horror story. At this point, I had been socially conditioned to think of myself as a bad person. After so many years, the mind becomes conditioned, based on all the information it's been told. Mine was conditioned to hate, resent and to see myself as this evil person I'd become. The hard part was that deep inside me, I still believed in an inner child, begging and screaming to be set free. I continued suppressing and ignoring the pain of this contradiction, even to the detriment of the only real children, my own flesh and blood, in my life. Sometimes, I fed this image of a separate child within through my self-pity. It took years to realize only God can love our innermost being, including the child we were.

We are all born to love but Satan takes us down paths that God never intended. While we can no longer be the child we once were, God can really be the father we all need; I have been reborn and again sense the innocence of my childhood.

Spring, 2004

Dressed in one of my father's sports coats, I arrived at the Bank of America building in downtown Dallas. This was the day that would ultimately determine my fate. My sentencing was a mere one hour away. My attorney, Lousie Grant of the prestigious and world renowned law firm, Hayes and Beezer, said to meet him at his office at "ten-ish." Immediately after easing from my car I was met by a parking attendant. "Ten bucks, sir," the man said as he whistled at another car and waved his hands like an air traffic controller.

I revealed three five dollar bills from my pocket, "Here 'ya go."

"It's only ten, sir."

"Keep the change," I humbly replied. This was a new type of tip I was giving, not for my own ego in flaunting my wealth but simply for a job well done. I was no longer wealthy, nor was I pretending to be. In fact, I was just off Food Stamps, living with my parents and borrowing my father's clothes. The big-wig corporate tycoon was just that, a big wig. Once the wig was removed, below was just another guy.

It had been literally three years at this point from the day my office was raided and Healthsphere was taken down. It was three years of watching an empire I had worked so hard to build die. Just because I was on the wrong side of the law doesn't mean that I didn't work hard. To see all of it fall as it had, then having the same sword hanging over my head, was a pain that cut to my soul. I brushed some wrinkles out of my dad's dark blue trousers, adjusted buttons for more breathing space and began towards the bank building.

Inside, I nodded at a couple of security guards, made my way up the escalators and then into the elevators. There were at least a dozen men and women who all jockeyed for position, waiting on the first available elevator to open.

"Thirty-seven."

"Forty-one."

"Fifty-five."

"Sixty-two," I said to the man who was suddenly in charge of everyone's destination. After a few stops, the bright neon numbers read, "62."

I took a deep breath and made my way into the large, thick, glass doors with the impressive Hayes and Beezer etched in the glass. There were hundreds of attorneys in their Dallas location, not to mention the paralegals, orderlies and wanna-bees. There was always a lobby full of clients, with women clad in business suits waiting on their every move.

"Rodd Brown for Louis Grant," I said as I leaned over the receptionist's desk. As I waited, my eyes became numbly fixated on one of the three large screen televisions in the lobby. I sat there just as indifferently as most of the others waiting, watching events on CNN. The redundancy, the endless powerlessness, was killing me. I distinctly remember picking up the USA Today hoping to find something fresh to occupy my mind with, perhaps something positive. I began thinking about the state of affairs in which we lived. My situation had an eerie echo to many of the current events I was reading or hearing about in the news.

"Ex-USA TODAY reporter faked major stories." Jack Kelley fabricated substantial portions of at least eight major stories, lifted nearly two dozen quotes or other material from competing publications, lied in speeches he gave for the newspaper and conspired to mislead those investigating his work. Kelley's most egregious misdeed occurred in 2000, when he used a snapshot he took of a Cuban hotel worker to authenticate a story he made up about a woman who died fleeing Cuba by boat. The woman in the photo neither fled by boat nor died and a USA TODAY reporter located her that month. His antics put her at risk of ever being able to immigrate to the United

States.

So much for getting a lift from my own troubles. The world is going to hell in a hand-basket, I thought to myself. Then, I thought about how I would have reacted to the exact same headline three years earlier, prior to the Feds bringing me down. The sad truth is that I would have laughed at the guy because he was so stupid as to leave a trail that would get him caught. I looked at those around me. For the first time, that morning, I began realizing I was playing the fool. The stupid things we think! It was so easy to keep up the sham once it started. I thought it gave me an edge against my competitors. Imagine how hard it would be if those same competitors could have read my cheating mind. Yet, I was unwilling to admit the Lord knew my mind better than I did. In the end, what we hide is going to be found out.

Enron and that whole debacle, was only four hours south of where I now stood. My first attorney, Joel Bernstein, said my case would be, "swept under the door because of the guys in Houston and now Mississippi." Joel was referring to the Enron and Worldcom scandals. I certainly felt like I was about to be the rug, though and about to be hung out to be beat! Here I was waiting for another lawyer, Louis, to try to fix things for me.

Louis was running a few minutes late, as I was informed he was on a phone call with the U.S. Attorney, Spikes. The knot in my stomach grew. I knew this could be either good or bad.

Nevertheless, we meandered through the winding halls. Of the many people we passed on our way to the conference room where I would discuss my fate with Louis, one wise looking man who seemed like he would be more at home brewing a very dark and thick beer or growing popcorn somewhere in the Midwest greeted me. "Morning, sir," he said, dipping his head as he spoke and walked.

"Having a good day?" this stranger asked me.

"Not really."

"It'll get better young man," he said as we passed. He paused, in the opposite direction. "Bad days get good and good days get bad."

God places people in our lives to provide for us just what we need when we need it. For the rest of my life I'll wonder who this man was. We continuously need to both minister and be ministered to. An interaction as small as this was something that not only did I need then but also has stayed with me, in holding great meaning for years now. Back then, I was left in the conference room unsure about what to do.

I crammed my hands in my pants, took a deep breath then just stared through the windows. The USA Today article was still on my mind, as odd as it may seem. But sitting sixty stories above downtown Dallas watching the ants busily carry out their daily rituals, striving to be something more than an ant, I was suddenly feeling differently about life. In place of my panic, something else was getting a hold of my heart.

Adultery websites!

Violence in the Middle East!

Corporate Fraud!

Domestic Violence!

Aggravated Assaults!

Family Feuds!
Civil Wars!
Democrats against Republicans!
Methodist versus Baptists!

People everywhere are trying to buy a win at all costs. The result is that no one can afford to win at any price.

I didn't know it but I sat just a few minutes from accepting a plea bargained sentence to prison. Staring from sixty-two floors up certainly put things into perspective. "Mr. Brown," Louis said as he walked in.

"Hey Louis," I said. "Why so formal today?"

"I was on the phone with Stokes. He said he would recommend the minimum to the judge."

"That's good news."

"Yes."

"How much will that be?"

"The judge has his own discretion but the recommendation will be around a year or so."

"Better than what we expected."

Louis agreed, then said he'd brief me on the way to the courthouse, which was right across the street.

Miraculously, Louis had taken my case after I was dropped by my first legal firm (which was another example of corporate greed); despite not being a criminal attorney, Louis did wonders. In fact, Louis specializes in environmental law and was used to dealing with corporate scammers not entirely different than me.

Nevertheless, Louis and I, along with a small team of attorneys he had assembled, walked across the street to the Earl Campbell Federal Building and into the infamous Judge Barefoot Sander's (appointed to the federal bench by Lyndon B. Johnson in the late sixties) courtroom. We all gathered in a pew near the front, then a few minutes later, I noticed my mom, dad and brothers entering the court room. What were they thinking of their boy?

After a couple of hours of idle paperwork and Louis discussing terms with the U.S. Attorney, I was sentenced to thirteen months in prison, with three years probation.

I would begin serving my time on July 8, 2004. I was told to show up at prison no later than 2 PM.

As I've learned.

Real forgiveness, as I see it, is the complete remission of our sins. It is only through forgiveness that we find what has been lost and save ourselves the grief of losing it again. I was once told by a preacher that I can never truly love until I can completely forgive. The inability to forgive poisons our souls and kills us a little every day. For me, finding forgiveness means overcoming my pride. Many times we won't forgive because we are so caught up in how we were "taken" or "fooled." We beat ourselves up for letting someone else get the better of us, in whatever fashion. This is where forgiveness can truly set you free. This is where you need to forgive yourself for not being more savvy, aware or strong. We are human and we are imperfect, obviously. But guess what? We are still loved and will be forgiven if we only ask. This can happen always and forever if we ask God.

It's a crazy thing, this concept of forgiveness. We can be forgiven without really having changed our actions. That requires only remorse. However, my remorse was always results oriented. I landed in prison, so of course I was sorry, not for my actions so much as having to pay the price for them. I was strong-armed by people higher up the Medicare food chain than I was, for skimming a bit here or there. Darn right, I was remorseful for that. Had I not been caught doing anything wrong, I would never have felt the need to be remorseful. Now at long last I'm beginning to understand that it's my own actions for which I need to be remorseful. Truly knowing that I'm sorry is changing my behavior.

I have been through anger management classes several times. It's not easy for a guy like me to swallow his pride and walk into an anger management program. I've got a lot of bad company. It's probably as difficult, if not more so, than walking into a drug rehab clinic. I could blame the drugs for my out of control behavior. I was an addict. I was not responsible, the drugs were causing me to be out of control. Yeah, right. No one ever forced me to take drugs when I began years earlier.

When emotions are controlling our behavior, it just feels downright unmanly to stop and acknowledge wrongdoing and only creates a deeper anger waiting to come out. What I didn't realize is that my emotions were a drug. My anger gave me a high and I became addicted to it. My body knew how to deal with anger, vent the rage, romp and stomp on anyone who got in my way. Depression, anger and despair are habits.

They can be addictions in and of themselves.

As I reflect over all my wrongs, I find that a lot of times in my life it's been easier to forgive others than to ask for forgiveness myself. This is because we judge others more quickly than we judge ourselves. Many criticize Christianity as a guilt driven religion. I don't agree with this. Our God is willing and ready to forgive us, His love is never beyond the reach of our arms. He was there through all my years of rage just as my own loving father was with me through every step of my journey. Just as I saw the tears my father wept every time he came to see me in prison, I know that God weeps every time we choose to go down the wrong path. Forgiving others is also easier, sometimes, because we don't need to accept the responsibility for our actions. Forgiving ourselves or sincerely seeking another person's forgiveness requires that we not only take responsibility for our actions but also acknowledge we need to change.

Admitting I had a problem was the first step. This is the first thing a newcomer must do in Alcoholics Anonymous. The reason this is the first step is to truly force the addict to say, "I am not in control." We realize that our addictions include our desire to maintain order and control, often lacking in our lives. It's only been in developing an unwavering faith in God that I have been able to truly say I'm not in control and that's okay, because God has a plan for me. I'll let Him keep control and try to enjoy the ride with all its ups and downs.

My past has made me a better human and more importantly, a better Daddy to my little girls. I have learned what it means to not only love God with all my heart, soul and mind but also to actually live it! When men and women love us as God does, they forgive us everything, even our crimes. We need to be careful here, because when a person hasn't dealt with their emotions, as I hadn't, seeking forgiveness may be only a tactic to manipulate a situation back into your favor. It's no different than a three year-old hitting his friend and upon being removed from the situation for a timeout says how sorry he is. He is sorry all right; sorry for not being able to play anymore. Empathy is the key here, understanding how our actions affect others and caring about that result.

It took a great level of tough love on the part of family and friends and federal prison in order for me to understand exactly what I needed to let go of. I had become such a master of using my fear and anger to control others, I even convinced my wife to remarry me! Yes, I used the concept of begging forgiveness to get what I wanted, although I hadn't changed one iota at that point. What I wanted was to change my circumstances, not myself.

Please don't misunderstand me, there were many who showed me an incredible amount of love and forgivingness along the way, specifically everyone in my family but until we are free to forgive ourselves and accept responsibility for our own actions, we will never experience the amount of life we are offered.

I had to do the work and dig deep inside to realize what it was that I was afraid of, before I could not only admit my true feelings but to deal with them. Then the real work began. I needed to learn to constructively communicate my desires, my fears and my needs to those around me. When you are in prison, you have to trust those who befriend you. The reason inmates feel as if they are fraternal brothers for eternity is because of the known fear we all experience when we are inside. If you are not up and up with people, you will find your time to be the most difficult of all.

Peace came to me in prison for many reasons. One of the most poignant was that I had lived my life as a fraud and in prison I was no longer faking. I had been found out by the Feds, by my friends and family and finally, by me. The incredible freedom comes from realizing we each have the ability to finally accept a personal self; the self that watches and feels life. I have become powerfully impressed by our living soul and the way it is strong enough to handle the revealing of our faults. I'm no longer afraid to be real.

There is a poem by Kristone that has a line, "I cannot hide myself from me, I see what others may never see." The truth is that I did hide myself from me or at least I tried. Deep down I began to at least know who I was and what I really was. My emotions told the true story daily. If I were to re-write that poem, I would say, "I cannot hide myself from God, He sees what others always see!"

Now I know that everyone around me sensed my veneers. God certainly knew it. My soul did as well but it wasn't until strangers forced me to be labeled as a fraud, that I could finally begin to be me. This was to become the most liberating experience of my life. This is where I could finally start letting go. Instead of trying to push harder, I was being pulled up from my abyss.

Chapter 8

In Shock: The Inmate

I know there are lots of people who will read a book about crime, wanting to be shocked. Yet, with the same sense I had of my life being stopped while in prison, there's so much pure grief in describing prison; it's almost impossible to put into words. It's not only shocking, to be in prison; it's revolting. There are disgusting and dehumanizing events, which sear a human soul. So while I am still learning to describe all the things about prison life in a book, it's not necessarily what this book is all about. This is why I think such great leaders and teachers, like Chuck Colson, can do so much good. Colson went from being someone who literally put words into a president of the United State's mouth to being called "inmate." There are many people who make fun of people 'finding religion' on the inside. But now, I've been there.

My first day in prison is probably forever etched painfully into my memory. I arrived at FCI Ft. Worth on July 8, 2004, at ten minutes 'til 2:00. At 2:01 I would have been a fugitive. I made sure of the timing and even regretted the loss of ten minutes of freedom. When I was losing my freedom, it was like losing my old life. Whatever else it is, prison is a crime against criminals. Think of it as instant payback.

I had been briefed on what to expect but those were only to be formalities. Prison is the difference between reading from a book and getting hit in the head with a book. As a first-time inmate, there was no sense of hope or wonder about it. I was just plain afraid to go in and yet more afraid if I didn't. I was met by two guards, with one on each arm. Did they think I would change my mind and try to run? More likely, it was to make sure there were no scenes or missteps. At the least, it was proof I was no longer in control. They whisked me through one large metal door with an ugly metal sliding "snap" behind us. I was behind the fence now and really scared to death. The guards had nothing to say; well, almost nothing, except for one smart ass (excuse me) who said, "Welcome home, we've been waiting for you." The other guard laughed. Does it make me less of a man to admit I never had one day without fear from that day? Before then, I saw myself as tough and ready to scrap or fight to be on top. Something inside me was dying.

I was taken down a very long sidewalk that seemed to go down two stories. At the door, one of the guards pushed a button and beeped inside. "It's Carter and Jenkins, we've got inmate Brown." The door popped and then opened. There were inmates in there, orderlies, keeping their heads down. This was the business end of prison, Shipping and Receiving. It's the room where the start and the stop of prison climax. For me, the beginning. I had already thought of the day I would be leaving, a thought that would linger my entire time in prison. Some prisoners take their time easily. I didn't. I wanted out from there every day I was in. Regardless of what I wanted, I was stripped naked and put into a cage, or holding cell, a small grid with bars all around it. My mind was numb and my body unresponsive. I was like a poor dumb animal, in shock. Then after an hour or so, I was given a baggy pair of spandex Khakis, white shirt and bright orange deck shoes. I would wear these prison trappings until getting suited with proper khakis, which would be another three days.

They took my pictures. Asked me questions. Rolled my fingerprints. And I was served my first prison meal in there. The taste is still with me. Disgusting. It was the worst meatloaf concoction I could have ever imagined. The food in prison was horrible. I had no appetite but ate as much as I could choke down because I wanted to stretch every second into a minute off my sentence. Eating the lousy food ticked the clock of my fears away. Now, when I hear of people with eating disorders, I understand a little bit of what they are hiding from; their fear in the future. I shuffled out of that place and into the compound.

Hours later, the Austin Unit counselor, named Buckwater, came and got me. We walked across the compound and into a very large building. It was a sad thing to stare at, this human warehouse, especially for anyone who had read about the promises of heaven and a mansion with many rooms. I wonder if hell has FCI as its own version of a mansion!

This portion of prison housed the San Antonio, Houston and Austin units. Austin was the fourth and fifth floors so we began climbing stairs. I had been given a pillow case with two sheets, one blanket, which would be my linen for the next year. Certainly different than the thread count I had grown used to.

In the Austin Unit, we walked down the hall, passing inmates who simply nodded their heads and kept the proper distance to a new inmate. They had seen it all before. We walked into the guard station or, as I came to know it, the cop shop. I was assigned a bunk in the day room, among thirty nine other inmates. There was no fresh air. The air there was rank and it was very hot. Inmates draped wet towels over their heads or across their shoulders. The smell was worse than any locker room I had been in and the noise was like none I had ever heard. Heckling. Shouting. "Fuck you! Your mamma! What's for chow!" I was shown my way to where I was to bunk and Buckwater simply said, "You're on your own, inmate." I had never been that scared before in my life. Only one event since then has scared me more. The learning curve was immediate and drastic.

My cellie, as they call your bunkmate, was a black guy name Clarence Clark, better known as Bay Bay. Blacks didn't hang out with whites, per se, but for some reason, Bay Bay befriended me that day. Here was someone who with a single word could have gotten me killed or just kept me petrified for an entire year; instead of hell, God had given me a friend who looked out for me as a brother. Isn't it a strange thing how strangers outside of prison, with nothing to gain by it, can be so petty? Bay Bay taught me the most by his decency. No questions asked. And I wonder if God was ever closer to my unexpressed, perfectly open heart, than when I was most afraid on that first day in prison?

Summer, 2004

I had been in prison for three weeks and things were beginning to make sense, if accepting being trapped can make sense. I was beginning to learn my way around the compound, which was spread out more than eighty-eight acres. Freshly manicured by the inmates, of course. The grass was perfectly groomed, sidewalks were spotless, fresh paint on every wall and the stair wells sparkled. There were 1,999 inmates; plus me. I was still looking at the world as me and them. Our job was keeping the facility in tip-top shape year round, twenty-four seven, three-hundred and sixty five days each year.

Austin Unit was intimidating. The halls were stark white and very long, lined with cells, continuously matched on both sides of the hall. The long hall emptied at the end into the day room, which was now a makeshift prisoner pod because of over crowding. Past the day room, the hall continued to left and right and each split emptied into a ten-man pod and on both sides of the pod were two-man flats. Inmates were stuffed in every nook and cranny.

There was an early Saturday morning, I have reason to recall. Saturday meant there was way too much free time. Some inmates, the lucky ones who handled prison like a fast food drive-thru, enjoyed the free time. But I had already learned that it offered way too much time to think.

I had just come back from the track, where I had jogged a very slow five miles. I was making my way down the hall and toward my bunk. Bay Bay was a very heavy sleeper (his own antidote to boredom) and this morning was no different. His sleep pattern was very odd. He would lay on his back and pull the sheets over his head and tuck them tightly beneath him. Being a turtle in prison could keep you sane; and safe. He would hardly move a muscle the entire time he slept. And there he was, wrapped like a tamale on his back. I walked around the bunk and began twisting the metallic lock on my locker. My thoughts were interrupted by shouting from the inmates. "Boss is in the house! Boss in the house! Boss is in the house!"

A few inmates were heckling somewhat loudly but not enough to be heard in the cop shop. "He's coming! Get it clean!" they were saying.

I had no idea what was going on, so I turned to figure out what was happening. Bay Bay immediately perked up and told me the "boss" meant the warden was in our unit. Bay Bay was out of his turtle's shell, jumping from his bunk and making his bed within thirty seconds.

Bay Bay told me not to stare. Don't draw attention, whatever happened. Only speak to the warden if he speaks first. My heart was racing like a freight train for some reason. The warden, huh? It was a stark comparison for me, who realized what I had thought was power over others was just grains of sand through my hands.

I'd seen them on television, of course and had heard stories since arriving three weeks earlier but I had never actually seen a warden – let alone my warden-in person. The fact is, wardens are allowed to be what Americans fear the most, a dictator. If you're lucky, you get a great man. And if you're unlucky, the warden makes prison as bad as most dramas paint the worst prisons. In other words, minute by minute hell.

I could hear a large set of keys dangling from the hips of the two guards that followed him. Then suddenly there he was, appearing in the day room. It's very bizarre, the awe a warden inspires. A warden commands rock star status.

"Which one is he?" he asked. He was wearing nice slacks, a blue pin-point Oxford, a paisley tie with the collar unbuttoned and both sleeves rolled up to his elbows.

"That's him," said Tolberson, as he pointing toward me.

Shit! What now? I wondered. Maybe Tolberson had pointed at Bay Bay.

Sure enough, though, the warden made his way toward my bunk. Bay Bay flinched nervously. I thought I was going to throw up!

"Which one of ya's Brown?"

"Me, sir."

"Come here."

Bay Bay whispered, "Keep it straight."

"Yes sir," I said, standing at attention in my grey sweats and white t shirt.

"Brown, how long you been in here?"

"Three weeks, sir."

"Three weeks, huh?"

"Yes sir."

The other inmates gazed on like lost sheep. Not a sound could be heard and both televisions had been turned off.

"Where 'ya working?"

"For Ms. Radist, teaching GED, sir."

"Well, I want you working for me."

"What do you mean?"

"I've decided to make you a trustee, Brown."

"A trustee?"

"Yip."

"OK." What else could I say? I had no idea if I was in trouble or something good was happening.

"You'll start Monday morning."

"Yes sir."

"Be at the back gate at six-fifty."

"Yes sir."

"Jones is your boss. He's a good man."

"Jones?"

"Yip. I've already notified Radist that you're changing jobs."

"Great." So much for asking me. Another reminder, expertly delivered. "You'll be working for me, my house, the bank, don't let me down."

"I won't, sir." Let him down? What did that mean?

He turned and began walking out of the day room. Without looking back he asked, "You won't be running, will you Brown?"

"No sir."

"I didn't think so."

Within a few minutes, the televisions were back on and the noise level immediately rose back to chaos.

Bay Bay slapped me on the back in congratulations as I made my way back toward my locker. It was overwhelming. I had no idea it was coming and now I was a trustee. From the way every one was reacting, I knew something significant had happened. Was all my time here going to be so clueless?

Funny though, I realized I hadn't deserved any trust for years. Now, three weeks into the system and I was being trusted. Why?

As I've learned.

The reality for me is that I will probably forever be a convict, no matter how many years after I got out of prison. Anyone who has done what I have done means constantly proving yourself. Even more than that, I also know my only true hope to stay forgiven and straight, is in the hands of Someone who can forgive everything. Sometimes, I almost feel lucky I was so messed up. How many people just have a few problems and so spend their lives being able to hide their secrets and never have to face needing forgiveness inside prison walls?

My life is now letting other people believe in me, know that I'm real, that God truly does have my heart and to allow them to trust me for the first time in twenty years, as the warden did.

As they said in every rehab and as my face shows the stamp of:

Trust is the first to go and last to come back.

Chapter 9
Daddy, Father: Which One?

There is little that I can think of that is more gratifying than having held my newborn children in my arms for the first time. So how could I have been so stupid not to go on being there to hold my babies, over the years ahead, when they needed me the most? Sometimes, we take how we feel about our kids as the meaning of love. Really, this is a bit backwards. We need to do more than love a feeling. We need to feel love. Love lets us feel, because love is all about actions; the things we do, regardless of how we feel at the moment.

I have always felt very close to my family; having a perfect family of my own was certainly a goal. But I got lost in creating the portrait of a life, as opposed to embracing life as it came along. Instead of having a thousand beautiful moments and a million memories with my girls, I became a sideline father, leaving everything involving parenting to my wife. Because of this, I had missed most everything special in my daughters' lives. In a real way, I crippled part of my life irreparably. For a long time, I excused what I did out of love and my desire to be the best provider I could be. The reality was that I wanted people to see me as a good provider, meeting all external needs. Instead, I provided nothing but a bad example. I threw tantrums, instilling fear throughout our house and zero emotional nurturing.

A hard lesson is to pray my babies will be loved and nurtured by my ex-wife's new husband. This doesn't relieve me of responsibility; it's actually another responsibility. God, how I wish people could spare themselves this kind of painful lesson. In spreading selfishness in the name of love, we end up with the potential of bitterness and loss. But we absolutely must hope for the best for our kids, no matter how it can be achieved.

Winter, 2004

I remember when my girls came to visit me in prison. My heart was racing out of my chest. Anxiety and other emotions were running through my mind. Literally, my palms were sweating and my forehead was drenched. There was sweat soaking through both armpits of my khaki shirt and down my back.

There I stood in the Austin Unit on that Saturday morning, staring through the windows and past Interstate 20. The cops cleared the intercom system with the usual three loud beeps to get the inmates attention and to quiet the unit to a hush.

"Listen up! Inmates Cook! Jones! Davis! Brown! Garza! Report to the visitation room immediately! You have a visit!"

Nervously, I crammed my hands in my pocket and took a quick glance in the small, plastic mirror that was on the door of my locker. I quickly wiped the sweat from my brow and as much of the anxiety as I possibly could. The cops cleared the intercom, again. Beep! Beep! Beep!

"Cook! Jones! Davis! Garza! Brown! Report to visiting room immediately! The compound will be closing in five minutes! You will need to get there before it closes!" they barked at us.

The nerves went well beyond the fact that my innocent little girls were visiting their daddy in federal prison for the first time. The fact was that up until now, I had meant little more to them than a picture on the refrigerator and sadly, I knew little more of them than what was told to me by Cari or my parents. Suddenly, I was Daddy. This was real and I never feared being rejected more in my life!

Coleman, the unit cop that morning, opened the large metal door and I raced down the five flights of stairs and across the compound, rehearsing over and over and over again, in my mind, what I would say when I first see Mica Lynn and Olivia. "It's good to see you both," I replayed again and again but that didn't sound right.

"I have missed y'all."

"How are y'all doing?"

Nothing sounded right. This should be natural and easy, these two living beings are my flesh and blood, yet a moon rock would have been more familiar to me at that very moment. I had seen them a few times since being indicted but nothing either will probably remember. "How was the ride here?" I thought as I tried to keep it very simple and generic.

Of course, I could always mention how much they had grown and how pretty they were. "My goodness, you girls are beautiful."

Or, I could actually hug Mom and Dad and sort of let the girls blend into a sort of fake, jovial chaos that I would create. For a guy who was a charismatic leader and a master of fraud, I knew that there would be no way of faking this moment. Kids are smart and mine would know if anything I said was from a false heart.

I would think of something, I had little doubt. At the door of the visiting room, I knocked and waited patiently. Metcaff, the cop at the door, opened the door and asked, "Name and number?"

"Rodd Brown. Inmate number 31395-177, sir!" I barked in a military fashion.

"Anything on you? Jewelry? Comb? Watch?"

"This necklace," I said as I grabbed the chain and pulled it from my neck.

"Is that it?"

"Yes sir."

Metcaff closed the door behind me and then unlocked the one that led to the visiting room. "Good luck," he said.

Inside the visiting room, I saw my dad standing across the room, my mom next to him and the girls were holding Mom's hands. The girls had their backs to me as I walked across the room and handed my identification to Sergeant Alambar at the desk.

My dad's lip quivered when he first noticed me. As usual, he had a Diet Coke in hand to distract from the emotions and cover the tears when he was around me. He immediately tilted his head back and began gulping.

Mom looked at me and smiled. Mica Lynn and Olivia both turned around and just stood there. Neither knew what to do, much less who I was. They simply knew me as their daddy and that was it.

I've heard stories of people who were put up for adoption who sought out their biological parents. Almost always, they ask just prior to the meeting if they will have that innate recognition of their own flesh and blood. I guess this would be the best way to describe what was going through my head. I stood there that morning, dripping wet and scared to death. This was suddenly very real.

My girls, my little angels just stood there in sheer terror. Mica Lynn was a mirror image of me and Olivia had the whole "Brown thing" working just as well. There was absolutely no denying they were my girls. None!

The only thing I could think of that morning as we all stood in the prison visiting room at FCI Ft. Worth, were the words I called their mother when I learned of her pregnancy, both times. "Bitch" and "Whore."

Had I ever felt more ashamed than hearing these words echoing in my mind, while looking at those girls?

Never.

As I've learned.

I am so ashamed for many of my actions. There are many things that I will never be able to take back. Those who are closest to us are the ones that we hurt the most and this damage is always the hardest to repair. They were looking at a man who they were expected to love just because I was their bloodline. I'm sorry but some things need to be earned and I hadn't earned it and I knew it.

This is not what my girls needed. The fact that I wasn't there to create a healthy relationship when it needed to happen and allowed so much of my own muck to cloud their innocent love for me, I am left wondering if I will ever be able to repair my relationship with them. They now live in another city and have another man as their father figure. In many ways, this is good; but the fact is that I am their father and I wish I could find a way to express my love for them that would not seem cliché or contrived.

Many guys inside prison understand exactly what I'm talking about. When Bay Bay told me to "take care of them girls," he knew that I needed to become a figure that my girls would be proud of, a positive influence in their lives. What they didn't need was to go through life with a stigma of dad being that dude who went to prison for all those bad things. Yes, I will always be that guy who did all those wrongs and paid for it; but I hope, as I grow, they will see that I have become a much greater man for it all. I hope that one day they will respect me and be able to make better choices knowing the lessons I have learned.

I will not buy their love with gifts and

indulgences. This was a large part of a portrait I was desperately trying to paint while I was sacrificing the most precious times of their lives. My awakening was seeing myself sitting in my new home, my car, debating the only solutions that were clear, fleeing the country or suicide.

For my own greed and desires, I had left my children behind. While I was in prison, Mica was already in kindergarten. I remember nothing pertinent of her pre-K years. Yes, I did pick her up from school on a few occasions and attended a dance class or two but I could not tell you whether her favorite color was pink or purple, if she liked to read or draw more and how well adjusted she was around her peers. I never stopped to talk to her teacher and ask the real questions to get the answers that parents want to know about their kids.

Just because I knew I physically had two little girls did not mean I was emotionally part of their lives. Nothing could have been further from the truth. If they were asleep by the time I got home, that was just part of being a dad for me. I was out providing, yet I wasn't paying attention to what I was really giving them: an inability to bond with me and potentially with other kids and people as they grew up. It takes more than just a mother to raise children. The influences of mom and dad are integral for any kid to develop a healthy self-concept. I was depriving my sweet little girls of this.

That morning, when I was in prison and my girls visited me for the first time, there were emotions running through me that I forgot I could even have.

Throughout my life, I always say, "This is the worst day of my life." But with so many "worst days of my life," it's very hard to categorize and quantify them. However, that morning clearly trumped them all as being worse than the raid, worse than the trial, worse than the sentencing. Forget the community backlash and my wife and friends deserting me, I deserved all that and more. As I stood there, I got the 'more.'

There is not another emotion in the world worse than that of your own biological kids not really knowing who you are. Having kids is easy. You don't need a license; you don't even need to be married. In a lot of cases, all you really need is a few beers and a few tender words, then it all starts. There is a biological purpose to sex: to propagate our genes for the survival of our species. What about the spiritual union between a man and a woman? We have lost sight of this and sex is not meant as a simple pleasure mechanism.

Often, if you're married, when you find out that "we're pregnant," you are happy as can be, at least for a while. The thought of a baby is heart warming and can fill some of the emptiness we feel in every other part of our lives. This is temporary, all too often.

At some point we realize parenting can feel like a job. In truth, parenting is not a job. Parenting is a tremendous responsibility. There are obviously costs involved. There are obligations of time and energy. As I read more and attended classes I really didn't want to be in, the addict's voice in my mind, almost a demonic possession, whispered, "Maybe I'm too selfish to tend to a helpless child but it's too late! I'm trapped!" Ultimately, my selfishness won over again and again and my needs superseded my children's. I put them in their figurative corner, the part of my life where they "belonged." After all, they did help to complete that social picture that I was desperately trying to paint; but I failed to keep them there, while doing things for them only as it suited my needs.

Taking my child to a dance class would not have any purpose for me unless there was a way for me to talk to someone and utilize the situation. I lost the joys in simply watching my child dance, the beauty of a pure soul expressing herself, her love of the world, of life and of me. I am hopeful, though. I do think that as my purpose has changed, my ability to see the joy and the purpose in my children has grown and my ability to take pride in my purpose as a father has developed.

Some of my choices have been more than difficult in this process. At times since the raid, I have chosen to keep my distance, in hopes of not exposing them to much of the stress and strain that goes on. My kind of fraud was not a kid's game and this level of stress is not healthy for girls to be around. The time that I do spend with them is filled with purpose now, to help them realize that no one is perfect, that Daddy is trying to make things right and that I will always be there for them when they need me. My purpose will not allow me to abandon my girls again.

As a result, I now realize that I need to do the same for my girls. I need to help them learn to make good decisions but more importantly to give them space to learn and grow and let them know in their hearts that Daddy is there for them, no matter what they do. After all, my kids were truly there for me, in complete innocence. I will always love them, though my earlier choices may not allow me to be the father I wish I could be. I am growing, I am trying and I hope, no, I trust they will understand.

When God finally delivered me, my girls were the first ones I ran to. In world record speed I ran to those girls and just began loving them. It took some time to build their trust but now we have an amazing relationship. Cari lets me see them whenever I want. That, friends, is God. Children look at you (at least if you're patient enough!) with genuine eyes. Be real with them.

Chapter 10

Next Stop: Halfway House

Bay Bay was the first one in prison to tell me about how my release from prison would go. He had already done this before so he knew the basic ropes. He talked about the difficulty. In fact, I had never thought about it until right now but Bay Bay was there on revocation. That son of a bitch was there 'cause the streets were too danged hard when he got out the first time! Just how hard it could be I was about to find out. And I had a thousand advantages, coming from a wealthy, loving family, that Bay Bay never had.

My worst days of prison were now ahead of me. It's a surprise, looking back, that those days weren't to actually be in prison. Someday I'll figure out how to write a book, just about my year in prison. For now, it's jumbled in my mind. More importantly, the story I feel called to tell has to do with me becoming forgiven. You see, the worst days were when I realized the ragged clothes I wore weren't my prison khakis. No matter how well I dressed, after prison there was a look on me and the word was always there, "Look out for this guy; he's a liar and a thief and an addict, just out from prison." I soon came to recognize or expect, looks of distrust when it came to people's money; when I first walked out of prison, it soon became obvious I was still not a free man. I had a long way to go before I surrendered. Though God had already opened my eyes, I had not yet surrendered my heart; so I was still in prison as far as paying my debts were concerned.

Summer, 2005

For me and I assume for most just-released ex-convicts, the last day inside is very strange. Even though you are about to be released, you're still government property. They begin prepping a person for release with about four months to go, hoping to make the transition easier, so there is a tremendous amount of anxiety involved.

The inmates haze you and those close to you have a "spread" where everyone throws in chips, salsa, cheese; and there's just this huge pile of nachos and those you are leaving behind are well-wishing. It's also hard to put into words, how to miss people who are your whole world, even though you can't wait to never see them again! Many of the people I met in there had years to go before their release. Celebrating (too loudly) getting out is a sure way to spread grief. Federal time is very long for most inmates and a twenty year sentence is pretty common in federal prison. They all wanted me to stay in touch, write to them and let them know what was going on in the world. When one of us got out, he was getting out for everybody. It was opening a door and getting some fresh air, if only for a second, "My turn's coming, my turn's coming." It wasn't until I was released that I was told you can't communicate with felons; at least, until my three years of probation are up.

Anxiety? Almost unbearable pain and excitement mixed. I was the kid who got sick at Christmas from sheer excitement. The guards came to my cell and got me. We walked across the compound and the inmates who were up that early, six a.m., started hollering, whistling and cheering. That send-off, at least, was very cool. It will always strike me that up until prison, my friendships had not been half as true. And here I was, leaving the ones that had become just what I needed. I had found making friends was a lot more profitable than making money. I wondered if I would ever make friends like these guys again. Roy Glover, Bay Bay, D Ray, Trissler; in reality, I was leaving the only friends I had. Small wonder so many people fall back in with criminals. For me, four years had passed since anyone wanted anything to do with me. I felt as alone and naked as when I had entered prison. What was waiting for me? Those people who wanted nothing to do with me, I was not ready to face. And those who had become my friends, I was not feeling ready to leave.

When I was in, a year seemed like a long time. Looking back and as I get older, a year seems like nothing. Again I'm reminded a bit of the stories of veterans. I have heard vets say a battle can last five minutes but doesn't stop for the rest of their lives. Though I was only in for one year, I also felt a sense of being institutionalized. This is a fancy way to say dehumanized. Oddly, there can be a real comfort in being less human and more of a thing. I mean, prison is a very safe place in terms of comfort levels. Routine becomes life and those inmates become your entire family.

Here's a comparison about leaving and it explains some of my feeling of confusion. It's like falling madly in love with a woman and then leaving her for no real reason, just leaving. Very hard to make sense of it, if you look for a reason.

Nevertheless, that morning we (two guards and I) made our way to Admin, where they cleared my books, gave me a new SS card and seventy-seven dollars that was left on my books. Money, that was strange as well.

There was the first smile, when I touched the money and unbidden came the verse, "Love of money is the root of all evil." Well, I had sure done evil for this love. It had been one year since touching money; and to think that seventy-seven dollars brought back the feeling, not unlike the millions I had made cheating. So I felt rich. But my priorities about money were going to be tested in the long months ahead. The only thing I wanted to buy with that money was Copenhagen and a Playboy.

We made our way back into 'Shipping and Receiving,' where it had all started one year earlier.

There was a box on a table, clothes my mom had sent in for me to wear to the halfway house. Levis and a Polo, wow. No more khakis.

After sitting in a cell for one hour, the guards finally ordered me to leave. Every emotion known to man was going through my mind, every single one: anxiety, fear, excitement, hope, helplessness, doubt. If they had pushed me back a step I could have just slipped back into prison because my legs had no mind or will to go anywhere.

Outside the fence, the other trustees were there waiting to hug me good bye. That was very tough but braced me up to get going. Never underestimate the power of showing you care when someone is way down. My boss, Ronnie Davis, was also there. We had all shared some very good times and it was time to say good bye to them, probably forever.

Then I saw them. Mom and Dad. They climbed out of Dad's truck and met me in the parking lot. Mom and Dad. Oh, did I want to cry then. I was carrying this huge bag with hundreds of cards, letters and pictures (proof that truly, we are a forgiving world) that I received while in prison. I dropped the bag and hugged my dad first, hard and long. Then mom. Then, finally, we all cried together as we made our way back to the truck and to Volunteers of America, the halfway house that would be my next stop along this journey.

It was an easy step, because within four months, my family trusted me with another opportunity. Unfortunately, it would lead to the most frightening step a person needs to make.

As I've learned.

To those who are suffering, you will be amazed at all the people who are trying to love you even when you won't accept their love. Addiction makes us selfish and can be an unbearable burden for those who love us.

My parents were always the ones to say to me,

"We still believe in you."

"We love you."

"You can make it."

"Don't quit now."

"I know it's tough but you're tougher."

Their words were always encouraging. I don't know how they did it, given the trouble I brought them but Mom and Dad were always strong in their faith and belief. They believed in their boys more than anything in the world and they would do anything for us, anything in the world.

We learned a new word in 1991, "enabler." While Todd was in rehab, his counselor told my parents they were enablers. I completely agree, yet had it not been for their unwavering love, there is no doubt where and how this story would have ended. I never threatened suicide to anyone but there were many nights had it not been for my parents, I selfishly would have taken my life.

So that's the word and the concept behind enabler is naturally very confusing to me. An enabler allows the person who is an addict to feel that the enabler will bail him out or put up with his addiction because of love. An addict, though, needs "tough" love; for those who love him to take a firm stand and tell him when his behavior is unacceptable, to refrain from bailing him out of his difficulties and to refuse to ignore his addiction. Many families, mine included, simply didn't talk about addiction. It was a bit like the old joke of the elephant standing in the living room, too big to ignore but if not talked about might simply go away.

The problem is, when do you stop enabling? I say that every situation is different and I can speak only from my own experience. I don't care what some doctor says who has never struggled, been addicted, or been to prison. Never give up on your kids, loved ones or friends. This is my guardian angel's message. I am convinced through my journey that there is a definite, definable point of loving and not enabling. Perhaps, my parents were enablers but when your heart knows only love, as my parents do, it's hard to stop. The best emotion my parents ever explained is that of love. People who are into their forty-fifth year of marriage know a thing or two about love. My parents loved me hard and long and never stopped. I do not, nor have I ever believed, that they enabled me to do the things I did out of weakness. I do believe recovery begins at a very personal and cognitive level. Whether the addict is surrounded by well-meaning enablers or not, the addict still has to decide he wants to recover. Enabling may prolong the decision and does in most cases; however, the addict or the one suffering has to make a decision to end his addiction. All the love in the world from others won't make matters better.

What's up with the word love anyway? We say 'I love you' and it flows easily off the tongue without a lot of real feeling behind it. It doesn't have much meaning when we use it so casually. Maybe we don't truly understand the meaning of love anymore. Maybe it's been lost through the generations. We don't really understand what love is, in the sense that my parents mean it. They grasp what it involves to really love someone. What it means to give yourself to someone else. We mistake friendship, commitment or lust for love; but God wired us a certain way to experience all that love was really meant to be, not to hold us back or to make us miss out on the best life has to offer. God created love and wants us to feel love as a total commitment to all that is good and pure in others.

Even after bringing so much trouble to my family, before and after the FBI raid, I say with gratitude that my family never wavered in their love for me, not once. Even during my darkest times, they stood fast and tall and offered me strength, while demonstrating their own belief that I had to accept the consequences of my actions. This is what I want to pass on. During the months after the raid and before my indictment, when my life was truly out of control, some of my parents' friends abandoned them because of me. I was too messed up to see all their love at the time. Looking back, I can see clearly how much they loved me and what that love cost them.

In fact, there were many times I told my parents selfishly that they didn't love me. After all, they weren't bailing me out of my latest scrape, a scrape that was far worse than any I'd pulled in college. That's a classic statement from an addict to put the burden on those around them to be responsible for someone else's bad behavior.

The reality was that I had succeeded at nothing I had set out to do. Sure, I'd created the illusion of success for myself, even while I knew in my heart that what I was doing was wrong, that it wasn't the path God wanted me to take. I'd harmed all those who loved me in the process but my vanity of proving myself to be a big man and a hero, came from letting pride control my actions.

To the mothers, fathers, brothers, sisters and friends of an addict who read this, I say, "There's hope." Let them know they need support and always show love. By not confronting your loved one who is an addict, you become one more enabler allowing them to continue their downward path. "Enabler" is a powerful idea and it is true to form. Someday a better word will come up, though. At the end, people get disabled. Learn the difference between enabling and loving. I say all the time, "It's better to be feared into heaven than loved into hell" and "Yes you can stop anytime but when?"

Chapter 11

Rock Bottom: Hurricane Katrina

Getting out of prison is taken as a blessing. The fact is, I was a long way from being free of worry. I wonder how many of our problems we cause by fearing all the wrong things? It's been my experience in this century that everything you fear will come true. If I feared anything when I was released, it was fear of further disappointing my father. I had come to realize there was nothing more important in this world than earning my dad's respect; I shuddered to think about trying to buy his respect again. No, this was going to be much harder. I found myself being ashamed for two people.

It had been two months since leaving the halfway house and I was still getting acclimated to a world that I had literally forgotten. Everyone develops a certain set of coping skills for getting by in the world. To the extent I had been successful in business, I had no other survival skills except for what I had learned in prison. My life had been in a horrible spiral since the raid in 2001, so I was left with a frustrating sense of having to not merely reinvent myself; I had to invent a life. I had no wife, no money, no real job skills; I sure wasn't going back into medicare billing. Whatever else I believed, I was finding out I was still my father's son. I wanted nothing more than to repay the people I had hurt. But how? Those years in between then and now were for naught. I was simply surviving, breathing God's air and waiting for a miracle of sorts. The good news was the fact I was hoping. My faith was stirring, too, and almost was a living thing, keeping me going.

In every real sense, it had been four years since I had even been challenged with being a normal citizen, or human for that matter. Getting a job. Paying bills. Doing all the things that normal thirty-eight year old men did. Four years and some change.

It seemed as though the Dallas/ Ft. Worth metroplex had doubled in size. There were office buildings, apartments and strip shopping centers everywhere. Even Denton was unfamiliar territory. Loop 288, on the south side, seemed very bizarre. Home Depot had moved to the Loop, Old Navy, Wal Mart, Bed, Bath and Beyond, they had all set up shop on the Loop, which was pasture lands the last time I checked. Even more startling, Denton now had two Starbucks!

After being released from the halfway house, Mom and Dad agreed to let me stay at their house until I was able to get back on my feet. And to do so, I would endure more pain. After all those years of reckless living, I was getting very good at pain and suffering but the pain soon to come would trump all I had ever been through, no question.

I had no idea in prison that there would be more challenge ahead, obstacles and events that seemed harder than being in prison. It sounds funny to me now, when I think of prison in some ways as only putting my life on hold. Although I had opened myself to self-examination, forced my inner face to the mirror, I still wanted to cling to my sense of being able to rise to the top of any heap.

The reality for me is that I will probably forever be a convict even after getting out of prison and staying straight. Anyone who has done what I have, has to constantly prove himself again. Maybe, a long time ago, things could be forgotten. No longer. Every thing you do is written down somewhere. Imagine what it must be like to stand before God, Who knows the evil we have thought, as well as brought. For me, however, my family was there, again, to offer me a chance. Fortunately, God never stops knowing what's best for us. I was still in need of learning a valuable lesson about humility. When you intentionally cause harm, you've got to be ready to accept your lumps from the world, innocent or not.

Shortly after hurricanes devastated Louisiana and other Gulf states, my brothers and father became involved in relief efforts. They gave me the benefit of the doubt and offered me a chance to do well, by doing good. I was given the job to recruit people and send them into the region for the "Blue Tarp" project. By the time I got half going, I had recruited several hundred men and women who had given up jobs, left families and re-located to Louisiana and Mississippi, to make what we were all led to believe was going to be a lot of money.

My contractors made the day long drive to the region and then immediately began producing an amazing amount of work. They slept in tents, vehicles, on the ground and in FEMA-sponsored camps at night. Conditions were nothing to write home about, the food was horrible, there was extreme violence and conventional rules of politeness were no longer part of Gulf society. Not only had these people risked a lot to go down there but they lived in risky situations while they were there. Nevertheless, they did what was expected and produced enough work for everyone to get paid very well.

"Good job," said Dad. It seemed to me we had both waited twenty years for something good – and by that I mean decency – to happen for me. I thought this was finally it.

"I'm proud of you," said my brother, Todd. He patted my back and shook my hand. He was truly proud of me. And that felt awesome!

It was unanimous; I had done a great job. I had no idea that this would lead to the worst part of my life, counting even the time in prison and the rehab cycles. Encouraged, the next day I began recruiting more people, nationally. The word had gotten out on several union boards and my phone was ringing off the hook. I had become a hero but I was priming myself for a fall. I had squandered the honor that could have protected me.

Let me tell the bad ending, first. Nearing the end of their first month, contractors were beginning to angrily pack up what was left of their hopes and heading back to Texas with one guy on their mind: Rodd Brown!

The reason they were angry was that there was no money for their work.

One week had passed with no money. Frustrating.

Two weeks passed with no money. Weird.

We began getting phone calls from very angry contractors who wanted and deserved answers. I had no answers, just promises to wait. "It'll work out," I told them. No one had answers, for that matter. Naturally, my fingerprints were all over the deal since I was the one who recruited everyone and made the promises. Rodd Brown this! Rodd Brown that!

My background was enough for rumors to start flying and for good reason. I was only a few months out from prison for fraud, so if there's something shady going on, I was the perfect target, rather than (as Congress later investigated) the government's mess-up in hurricane relief.

Tempers were flaring and there were actual physical fights amongst contractors. Everyone wanted to know where the promised money had gone. I was called every name in the book. I was given every threat imaginable. I don't blame anyone. I understand where it was coming from. Fortunately, it wasn't true this time.

For the first time in my life, I had actually done something well, without cheating and it was beginning to feel like a back fire. It was only a few short weeks ago that we, Dad, Todd and I, sat in a mall parking lot in Denton, watching one hundred and fifty contractors set sail for the region. Dad and Todd were amazed at the work I had accomplished in such a short time period.

Now there were men showing up at Scott and Todd's office demanding money, answers and a shot at me. Suddenly, I was the bad guy yet again. The numbness I had felt for years began to return. I began feeling like nothing good could ever happen to me. I rolled out my old sound tape, as if I were the victim. I really felt that there was a dark cloud that was going to find a way to rain and thunder over anything I would ever try to do. It felt as if I were destined to return to prison and become institutionalized. Just as I had to be the biggest winner in my game, I was determined to be the biggest loser. Pride works to hurt us on both sides of life, up or down.

This deal with "Blue Tarp" had become so big, so quickly, that I had set up an office near Dad's. I was in business, fully operational, taking names and numbers. I said what I could to keep my pride in check but my head was swelling. I have to admit, I was quite proud of myself but it was all coming apart fast. Nobody had been paid and there would be hell to pay.

I would be the first one to pay.

Fall, 2005

I arrived at my office that morning and just sat in my chair, dumbfounded. It was way too much for me to handle then. Prison certainly seemed much easier than what I was going through that day. There was a knock on the door and I wondered, "What now?"

"Come in," I mumbled.

"Morning," said Scott as he made his way into the office. Scott was the implied "head of the family," not only because of his older brother status but because of his enormous financial smarts. Scott is very even-keeled, very well-respected and extremely successful. Consequently, he had been the one chosen to speak to me that morning. He seemed nervous, so I asked the first question, sensing something in the air.

"What's going on?"

Scott seemed hesitant to answer. "Oh, not much. Thought I would come by and visit," he said. He was visibly shaken and obviously holding back some tears. His mouth quivered as he spoke, "This is hard for me," he said then paused for a long second, "very hard."

"What is it?"

"This Blue Tarp thing ain't going well, as you know. There's a lot of mad people out there."

"I know."

"I mean it's real bad."

"I know."

"We've talked about it and I don't think Denton's a good fit for you right now." The tears made it hard to watch and hear.

"What do you mean?" I cried.

"It's just not a good fit for you. I just think with what you've been through and what you're going through now, it's just time to leave."

"You mean move?"

"Yes."

We both sat in total silence, tears and runny noses,

two grown men's sniffles, echoing through the tiny office. I can't imagine what it took for Scott to be there and say all this to me. After all, it was my family that had stuck by me, through every bit of wrong that I did. Now that my one good deed had gone bad, it was all too much for them to take. Sadly, I tried to understand and, at the least, respected his courage.

"You gave it hell, man. It just didn't work."

"Ok."

"Do you have any where you can go?"

"I'll find somewhere."

"I can help you with money or whatever until you get started. You're a salesman, you can get a job anywhere."

"I know."

"I feel bad but it's the right decision for our family. Me, Todd, Mom and Dad will be here for the rest of our lives and you won't. You belong in the city, like Dallas."

Though it was hard to hear, Scott was absolutely correct. It wasn't fair for me to jeopardize all the years of hard work the others had gone through to get them where they were at. Reality isn't always the easiest thing to take but the reality of what Scott was telling me was that they saw the length at which my wings would span if I would only open them. It was time to leave. My heart knew this. Maybe I had worn out my welcome long ago but I felt as if I had to set some things straight, at least with my family. I was beginning to grow up.

"You know I didn't keep the money, right?" This was the most important question of my life. What did the family really think?

Scott didn't hesitate or bat an eyelash. He said, "I know."

"You believe that, right?"

"Yes. It's just a bad deal and they're blaming you."

"This is hard."

"I know. You'll be better for it. I promise."

He had no idea just how much better I'd become, nor did I for that matter.

"Ok. I'll leave."

"When?" The urgency and fear in Scott's voice were obvious. I can only imagine people showing up at my brother's office, maybe harassing his family. I am certain the ramifications went well beyond my office and my phone line. On top of all that, I am certain that Scott expected the old Rodd, full of anger and resistance. This morning was different for me and for us both. This was the start of surrender but it was just the start.

"Today. I don't have much so I'll just throw it in my car and be gone."

"I appreciate it, Rodd, and I'm sorry."

I knew he meant what he was saying. I had created a mess and I wasn't nearly whole yet. Scott knew that. So did God. We hugged hard and cried even harder. By the end of the day, I loaded my car at my parents and headed south.

Though there would be more very hard times to come, I was at least taking the steps to become a man and do the right thing, regardless of how hard it had become. I remember driving out of the city limits and for the first time in a very, very long time, praying to God and asking questions. As crazy as it was, I had some sense of peace, though there were many unsettling things on my mind as well, peace loomed.

I drove for an hour or so, just praying to God. Finally, asking Him "What it is I'm here for; my purpose, my life and my existence?" For the first time in my life, I realized that for all those years I had simply existed, taking up space. There was no substance to my life, my heart or my soul, just air. I also realized that prison wasn't rock bottom for me. I wasn't even sure if this would be rock bottom. I also realized at that moment that when you think you're at rock bottom, you have two choices and these choices are now something of a motto to me; let it be rock bottom and begin climbing out or find out there's more where that came from.

"God, who am I?"

"You are mine, son."

"What do I do now?"

"You still have lots of growing to do. More struggles. I want you spreading a message of hope to people just like yourself."

"A pastor?"

"No. You will go door to door. Don't wait on them, many won't seek your help. You haven't proven yourself yet."

"When do I begin and how?"

"I'll leave that up to you. You will make a few more major mistakes and through them you will learn to trust only me."

I was confused and not sure what to do. "Any

direction?"

"Simply trust in me, son, I will get you through this. You have been blessed, you're just now realizing it."

"So . . ."

"That's it. Believe in me with all of your heart, soul and mind. Trust in me. Have faith in me and never stop!"

Easy for him to say, He's God. My thoughts were not convinced that I could do this. I was still homeless, friendless, broke and confused but there was a calling on my life; I simply had to find it.

They say that sometimes people we meet are the angels who God sends to us. When you are in times of need, you often find yourself taking routes you wouldn't normally take or trying things you wouldn't really consider trying previously. One week earlier, I had met a wonderful Christian woman, Molly Mills, on a Christian dating site. I called her and told her I needed to stay a few nights and, "I'll explain later." Reluctantly, Molly agreed. There is no doubt in my mind Molly was placed in my life for a reason, though I would cause more pain before realizing it.

Over the next three months, I started the hardest journey of my life; recovery from the mess I had created since graduating from Denton High School in 1985! It wasn't anything spectacular, almost phony; but it had the promise of being as great as anything I had ever done. I convinced myself that everything I was doing was right and pure. It didn't take long for me to wear out my welcome at Molly's. She had her own burdens, raising two spectacular daughters herself.

I was still faking my way along. She believed in all that she did. She could see that I hadn't completely surrendered to God's will just yet. Then she told me that. Molly made a few phone calls to the church and found a family, Gary and Sue Black, who agreed to let me live with them.

Finally, rock bottom? I was homeless and broke. Now, there was nobody left except two complete strangers, Gary and Sue Black. I certainly could only hope this was rock bottom. I couldn't imagine losing anything more but some smart guy once said it takes more than hitting bottom for an alcoholic to change. It takes looking up at the bottom of the barrel to admit, "I can't do it by myself."

I remember lying in bed, wondering and praying. "God, do you see what's happening?"

"Of course."

"Why?"

"You haven't surrendered all."

"Do you even care?"

"Son, I cared when you didn't, loved when you didn't, believed when you didn't."

I would begin the next day, climbing from rock bottom. There was a calling on my life and I was finally getting it, onward and upward with God.

As I've learned.

There is an old proverb that tells us "success is measured not by the accomplishments that we have but by the obstacles we overcome." This is a message that sounds wonderful, as we say it to our children but then demonstrates it is wiser to do as I say and not as I do. Then they grow up, often shut down communication from us and experiment with drugs, alcohol and sex. By the time we realize we are losing them or have the courage to confront the situation, it is usually too late. We have lost them. Certainly, we will have lost the bond that we once shared and bragged about to friends. In the worst cases, we have lost them as they fell to the world they decided to venture into well before they were prepared.

I hope one day I will be measured for the obstacles I have overcome and the strength demonstrated by my parents throughout my entire life. While I hope that my family and those in my community will see that I have truly changed my ways, I know that so long as I am walking with God, the right person will measure me properly. In that, I must trust that everyone else will follow His lead.

Most of us are doing the best we can. We try to live life according to the rules but get lost in a matrix of social and political quagmires. Some of us are more vocal about the deeds we do (I was), while others of us judge people for their simple ways. What we often miss is what is really important to God in the end.

Each of us has a calling, a vocation all our own. Some of us are meant to entertain people while even fewer others are called to lead a nation; yet others are drawn to the path where simplicity is the very essence of life. My point is that what we are called by God as our mission in life is seldom glamorous and seldom with great admiration of those around us. Most of us are entrusted to care for our children.

Our hearts know the difference and they are crying

out for help through addictions, rampant depression and illness. We have to live with ourselves. What transpires between God and us, especially if done with impure intentions, can never be rectified by accolades of our friends and family saying how great a deed we just did, "in the name of God."

If we want to be brutally honest with ourselves, we need to admit that we bear little resemblance of a church causing the gates of hell to shudder. God's plan is right before our eyes, yet we remain blind to it. Tragically, I almost squandered the awesome life God intended for one of His creatures. Most of us live in this horrible frenzy and fear of missing something, not being included, being left out, don't we?

At least I did, anyway.

God's plan made a hopeful beginning but man, myself included, spoiled his chances by sinning. Many will end in God's glory but, at present, the other side appears to be winning. We have bent so many rules and changed so much of the Biblical landscape that we have literally lost sight of the actual meaning of the Bible and the purpose of our lives.

Chapter 12

The Fight: Born Again

Facing my own battles, I wondered as well just how many battles for a soul take place every day? I've already talked about how skeptical I once was about angels, looking over us. I never thought, at the time, I would survive a fight to save my soul, let alone, tell anyone about it in absolutely certain terms. The battle I waged for salvation seems natural enough now. There had to be a fight between my instincts and conscience to avoid going back to prison.

Being truly released from prison and truly understanding recidivism came through talking to dozens of inmates, especially listening to inmates back in prison on revocation. I have come to the conclusion that punishment will hardly possess enough deterrence and power to prevent crime. Likewise, whatever the punishment, once a specific crime has appeared for the first time, it's reappearance is more likely than its initial appearance could ever have been, especially without God. This translates into a worry for me and for the more than a million other people who have been put in prison. Will we fail?

I would spend my year in prison, physically recovering from addiction. Sadly, I would never "die unto self," as I so desperately needed. In fact, one of the most successful prison programs in America has been shut down because it's sponsored by a religious organization! To my understanding this makes of punishment a life of prison. If there's no chance at redemption, of change, then the sentence can never fit the crime.

While in prison, I discovered all the things withheld from us and denied to prisoners as punishment, was exactly what we want, most of all.

I was already twenty years into serving my own, self-imposed life sentence, having learned nothing of great value. I was a proud man, a smart guy, who imagined I had all the answers. Obviously, I didn't. I convinced myself of entitlement to the easy life without understanding that my entitlements had nothing to do with money or material things. Real reward has to do with love and grace from a power much more intelligent than I could ever pretend to be. I know that I am not alone in how I perceived my "inalienable rights" as an American, a husband and a man.

Having been given no new life skills to reform me while I was in federal prison, I was released on May 13, 2005 (though I would spend that summer in a halfway house) with the same dark, callous heart. I started making phone calls to begin networking with the same folks I had done business with in the past. This was natural and comfortable. You would think that after a year to process, I could have come up with a different plan but the scope of prison life leaves little time and energy to plan anything other than surviving prison. I conceded that perhaps I'd become so lost that there was no way for God to ever touch my heart, change my ways and convert me. This became increasingly frustrating as I so desperately wanted and needed Him to do this. I still felt the yearning to be a Godly man. I still felt the battle between my will and my nature. My life seemed hopeless, wasted. My family wasn't speaking with me, after the hurricane disaster. Friends? My best friends were in prison.

At this point, I simply feared my past. Let me say it another way. Almost every doubt we have to do the right thing comes not from a present temptation. It comes from a fear behind us. We are somehow afraid that doing the right thing won't be enough, because of something bad that's happened in the past. For example, we whisper to ourselves about the relative ease required for to rebuild things from the ashes of our past. Since I now know what I didn't know then.

I had trained myself to think all I had been, was all I ever needed to be. Worse, I feared all I had ever been, was all I could ever be. Small wonder I described myself into thinking I was such hot stuff. There's the curse of has-been-ism. It's a place to hide from the future.

Despite being so far from worshiping God as my

Lord, I continued to have conversations with Him, seeking grace. It takes looking back at the path you just walked to understand that in those most dire times is when God is holding you up, paving the way, if you would only stop fighting him. My conversation with God that day was very methodical and very clear, I could not go back to my former life!

There was nothing about me I could hide from God. He knew exactly who was begging for help, bartering with whatever was close at hand with little more than a desperate intention. I had not been rehabilitated for the year I spent in prison, not even close. He was dealing with a man that was more afraid of who he was and what his own power was, than of the enemies he had accumulated over the years. For all the raw talent I possessed, I was unable to harness the power to make it for the greater good, partly because I could never relinquish my pride. Of the seven deadly sins, this appears to be most rampant in corporate corruption today, at least using me for an example, anyway. It is the value core of business greed and I was just as guilty of it as anyone else. I knew how to use my talents to manifest "more" of whatever it was that I needed.

I was scared and alone, living with Gary and Sue Black. The Blacks had been total strangers but accepted me into their home for reasons unknown then but very clear now. I remember specifically, quietly, asking God again, either to take my life or to give me enough strength and courage to continue living. These were the two stark choices; there was nothing more. This was the scariest moment in my life.

Winter, 2005

It was my first night at Gary and Sue Black's house in Plano, Texas. Amazingly, or sadly, yet another stop in the wreck of my life. Home now was a donated back bedroom in the rear of a house and a neighborhood I knew nothing about. The emotional fall was killing me. I had been reduced to living off the pity of strangers.

I knew the inside thoughts of suicide well. Not so much killing myself but wondering how much safer I'd be if I ever had the courage to end it. I don't know if I'd ever really be missed. I had all my worldly goods in one large, black suit case and a car outside. That was it.

My girls were back in Denton, living with my ex-wife and her new husband.

Todd was doing awesome in business.

Scott was still King Kong of Denton business.

Dad was the only one with any hope in me, though it was fading fast.

Mom was simply spent and jaded, though she prayed for me all the time.

I was essentially a favor away from homelessness and a likely return to drugs.

And constantly I felt the ache of frustrated wishes, hopes and success. From a world of wealth and options to living a life I could not conceive as worth continuing.

I fought like hell to get to sleep that night. My heart was racing. I just couldn't believe the mess my life had become.

I couldn't recall the last time I laughed. I couldn't

remember the last time I spent time with friends since leaving prison. I couldn't remember anyone even saying my name without bashing it or running me down. In fact, lying there in the dark, I couldn't remember a whole lot, as though my life was so much sand, washing away in the night.

Molly Mills, one of the most courageous and God-fearing women I have ever known, who took me in after being run out of Denton, was the only person on Earth who wanted anything to do with me after the Blue Tarp fiasco and she had now "pawned me off" on the Black's. Boy, would I regret this thought, the next day. I knew the Blacks had gotten in way over their heads with me and I also knew that if this didn't work, I would seriously blow my head off.

I was the most awesome salesman in the world and that night I wondered if I had strength and sell enough to convince myself and the Blacks I was worth the trouble.

I had books written by great authors scattered across my room, though none of them helped.

What do you mean, today is an awesome day? What do you mean, think positive? And what in the hell do you mean, rejoice if struggles and hard time! What in the hell do you mean preacher boy? I read the jacket and I never saw prison, rehab, divorce, poverty; nothing for god's sakes! So what makes you think you can tell me pain and suffering is safe and ok?

One of the books had been written by an author who had gone through divorce and was "emotionally distraught." Wait, my doubting mind said, this was the same preacher who just two books ago was telling me that "God brings pain and suffering in our lives and that we should rejoice in it!" Well, as my Uncle Don says with all of his simple brilliance, "Show me a sermon, don't preach it."

No problem here with those who preach, teach and share God's love and hope. But it's very difficult to hear it from those who don't live it. The ministry can be a very lucrative profession and, sadly, there is way too much money being spent on things besides helping wounded men. A pastor once said, "A Christian solider is the last man I want to take to the battle field with me." Wow. He simply meant many of those who claim to be Christians aren't good humans.

Those of great faith are well known, Billy Graham, Chuck Swindoll, Charles Stanley, Tommy Nelson.

So, with those books around me, I had this innate sensation that God was trying to talk to me that night. You know, as it turned out, I got more than I bargained for once I was willing to listen. Whoever thinks salvation decisions should be easy should not read on.

God had tried many times before and I had always used him as a rabbit's foot or a genie looking to get me through the right now.

I remember I just kept tossing violently in bed, nervously, not real sure what was going on. This was not just sleeplessness. I felt chained and racked to that bed; as though I was almost at sea in the bed. I'm telling you, I had a fever or something. It was very different than anything I had experienced before. Even the sleepless nights before prison could not compare.

So this may sound increasingly odd or way out

there but listen, there was a struggle emerging in my soul, a fight. I mean, literally, my body had to move to accommodate all that was going on in my soul. I would pull my knees toward my chest. Stretch my arms out. Roll over. Squeeze my fists together. Breath hard.

I thought, momentarily, I was having a very real heart attack but it was even more than that. Way more.

I cannot to this day accurately guess how long I wrestled myself while whatever was going on inside played itself out. And there was one stretch of minutes that were very tense, near the end.

I wanted to get up, tear loose from the grip of whatever was going on and dial 911. I would have to explain losing my mind but that was okay. Maybe, even get a prescription. But I just could not rise up. I tried. Finally, I felt even the possibility of getting some kind of "fix" lost it's appeal. The image of my family came to me and I realized I was through causing them pain. I would rather die than hurt my family again.

And this is what it takes to be born again; to face death of the old self.

They had been through plenty and a trip to the emergency room that night was not something they needed. Being taken away as a mental case would be too much an instant replay of my past to them.

If in fact it was my life to be taken, so be it. I began making things right with God. More accurately, God began to make me right. Like those who are sent to war and before leaving American soil, they get right with God. I did the same thing. I prayed with all my heart . . .

Dear God,

I know my life has been a mess. And I know the pain I've caused everyone. It was not my intention and I hope you know that. I hope you can forgive me for not being honest. I have wanted to be normal for a very long time. I want to laugh and love, just as those I see laughing and loving all around me. I am not a bad person but I have done bad things and for that I am very sorry.

Let Mom and Dad know they did the very best they could do for me. Do not make them suffer and lament over this very long. They are getting old, so let them have some peace about my life.

And Scott, let him know that he was a great, big brother. He was proof that whatever Mom and Dad were doing in raising kids, it worked.

Todd, this will shake him more than the others and just let him know that it was his strength, his love, his friendship that helped me to go on. He was my best friend and my soul mate. He will miss me the most, so please comfort his heart.

And God, please be with my baby girls. Though I haven't been a good father, they still know and love me. Let them know their Daddy wanted to be a good man who got caught up in a bad life.

Forgive my sins, all of them . . . please don't let me go to hell. Many people will believe that's where I'm at when it's over but please don't do that. I don't know exactly what to say to convince you, how could I? I just trust you as my personal Lord and Savior. I really do and I need your help to keep at it. Amen.

It was over.

And for some reason I went to sleep immediately, not very sure what would happen during my sleep, or if I would wake up.

I woke the next morning, more than a bit dazed. I looked around the room and I was alive. Really, truly, thrillingly alive. The sheets had all been strewn to the floor and that was fine, I was alive. More. I was reborn.

There was a feeling in my soul that morning that I had never felt before. I could feel my soul as a separate, loved part of my life. It was calm and there was peace. It was almost eerie.

But for the first time in twenty years, I had a comfort about being much more than just Rodd Brown. All the years I had reveled in being "me," were wiped away.

As I learned over the next few days, as I smiled, laughed and began being normal like so many other people in the world, there had indeed been a fight in my soul that night. A war of sorts. A civil war.

It was God kicking Satan's ass out of my heart and out of my soul, literally. God was reclaiming what was His and it took an all-out brawl to get it done. For who knows how long, that night, God fought Satan tooth and nail and gave me peace, my life.

My life had changed and God would begin the process of rebuilding. It wasn't going to be easy and it would take a very long time but it would be done because now, God had me. And that was very cool.

As I've learned.

Crime is terribly revealing. Our soul is revealed by our actions though we try and vary our methods as our will, our tastes, our habits, our attitude of mind and our soul whimsically follow any number of paths presented in false ambition. Until we surrender our will, our ways and our life to God, we will never find the right path or the security within our own character to embrace those gifts we are designed to use for the greater good of our fellow man.

God intervened for me, beyond any expectation I had from him because of my corrupt ways. He forgave me, lovingly. Miraculously and without warning or notice, God intervened and against all insurmountable odds, changed my life immediately and forever! God forgave my past and has since given me the awesome ability to love others, as He loves me.

Many people don't believe in stories like mine and that's fine. But people should stop to consider believing in experiences like mine. For me, I understood the mysteries of people who had survived suicide attempts or near death experiences. These experiences may tell me it isn't supposed to happen but it does, one amazing fight, not quite too late.

Chapter 13
God and Rodd: The Ministry

If you look back at the start of this book, as I look back at the start of my adulthood, you'll be able to see the biggest change in me is about people. I used to want to be in charge of people. It was my control trip. And my addictions, including my "show off" spending, were ways to buy people's affection. I spent respect, like it was water and drank up pride like it was air. Now I start my days wanting to be of use to God; I pray for people to use me up, so God can fill me up. The less of me, the more I'll be. The friendships and partnerships God provides me with have little to do with money any more and everything to do with the feeling of abundance and wealth I now have.

Here's a powerful example of a new friendship, I never could have realized if I hadn't been arrested. Since my release, I have made friends with a good loving woman, Donna Hope, whose son, Chris Hope, is serving time in the Clemons Unit in the Texas Department of Corrections for aggravated assault with a deadly weapon, in large part because of his addiction to Xanax the night of the crime. When Chris was arrested and searched, the cops found at least a dozen Xanax pills and quickly unraveled a prescription pill addiction, among others. Donna is a recovering addict herself who has been "born again" and is now on fire for the Lord. She has a gentle spirit and, like many parents, is dealing with choices her children have made. I remember the first time we spoke on the phone.

Donna asked in a very quiet voice, "What's it like in prison?"

"It's tough as hell," was my honest, sad answer.

"Is Chris ok?" She sounded shaken and frightened for her baby boy who was locked away at twenty-three years old for fifteen years in a maximum-security prison.

"He's got a few minutes left but he'll be fine. Give it to God." In prison, minutes are the measure of time, inmates referred to their sentences as "a few minutes" or if they were within one year of the door they would say they referred to the remaining time as "a hot minute."

"It's difficult for a mother but at least when I go to bed each night, I know he's alive. Prison saved his life," Donna said.

This was an insight only a woman who understands God's ways could have. Donna prayed on the phone that day. She prayed that her baby boy would one day come home and I remember her asking God to, "Protect Chris while he's away." I could only sit and listen as God ministered. "Will you write Chris if I give you his information?" she asked me.

"Absolutely!" There was no other answer for me.

I explained to Donna the importance of an inmate receiving mail. At FCI Fort Worth, mail call is every day at 4:00 p.m. All the inmates gathered around the lone pool table and listened hopefully, each one yearning for their name to be called. The cop dumped all the letters onto the pool table and began the tedious process of calling those inmates who had mail, one name at a time.

As I said to Donna, "You can be anyone you want to be in prison. Say anything you want to say about your life before prison. Brag about this or that but the truth comes out in mail call. Those whose families gave up on them get no mail. Those whose families haven't given up get cards and letters they will read over and over again, hanging onto every word for hours." Nevertheless, we spoke for a few more minutes before giving her my email address.

"Send me Chris' information and I'll get a letter in the mail."

"God is going to do amazing things in your life, Rodd Brown, there is no doubt about it," were her closing thoughts to me. He just had.

We hung up and at that moment, my ministry began; not a true ministry, per se, just my everyday life with God. My life was no longer just Rodd. It was now God and Rodd.

Summer, 2006

In crossing each other's paths daily, folks demonstrate how everyday miracles work. I feel profoundly for Chris and I feel for his mother, Donna. Both are going through their own personal hell. For Donna's strong wisdom and the perspective their journeys offered my life, my heart will forever sing a song of peace and praise for them both.

Below is the letter I sent Chris:

Dear Chris,

I don't know exactly what happened or the charges you faced, nor do I have a real need or desire to know. I simply want you to know there is amazing hope if you allow God to work in your life. I have been where you are, so I know the pain, loneliness, confusion, anxiety, isolation, fear and all the other emotions you encounter daily. I know them well, believe me. I remember waking many nights while in prison trying to piece my life back together and wondering where it all went so wrong and now, looking back, it was the best thing that has ever happened to me, bar none!

I know your life in prison is hard for anyone on the outside to understand and it's even harder for others to understand the daily ritual of being an inmate. Having only been removed from the system for less than one year, I now see both sides of the incarceration. It's a very delicate balance for all involved, no question. Just know that your mother is in constant prayer for you and has others, like myself, praying for you. God has a plan for your life Chris, allow him to work.

As I say, since my release and to many groups and individuals I share my story with, God takes men into deep waters not to drown them but rather to cleanse them. You must first sit still long enough to hear his voice and listen with ears that are amazingly sensitive to a new life and a better future God has for you.

Chris, there are only two options when you leave prison: either return on revocation or change your life completely through God's amazing grace. The first offers no solace; the second offers a world of peace, joy and love. I left prison in August and chose the latter. My life is now filled with incredible joy!

Chris, I am praying for you and I walk and share your pain. The good news is very simple: God has a plan for your life!

> *Amazing grace*
> *How sweet the sound*
> *That saved a wretch like me!*

The wretch in that song, that's me and you. God's grace is beyond belief. Be filled with it!

God bless you brother,
Rodd Brown

As I've learned.

For as long as I can remember, I knew that my life held a purpose much grander than I could ever imagine.

Surrendering my life to Jesus Christ has been a tough road but I have done it without reserve or regret. My conversion has been the most amazing experience imaginable and my prayer is that each of you can enjoy God's grace, His love and His forgiveness just as I have.

This isn't meant to sound mundane but I seriously feel that I am the most blessed man alive! For the first time since graduating from the University of North Texas in 1992, I am finally able to enjoy time with my family. My Mom no longer needs to send me letters stained in tears ending in "I love you and can't wait to see you this weekend, Mom." Dad doesn't have to answer his cell phone, publicly, to say, "Dale Brown," or punch in a code after accepting a phone call from a federal prison. Scott, enjoying a celebrity he so deserves and has worked so many years toward, isn't ashamed when he sees friends or colleagues who would invariably ask about his lil' brother. No longer does my brother Todd have to visit me in prison and just sit in the plastic chair, crying, telling me to "move on," "hang in there," "it's almost over," or "I love you, man." No, those days are gone and I'm finally moving on. I walk each step, take each breath and live each day like I have been blessed beyond my wildest dreams! My journey was their journey and now that I've found my way we can have the most incredible family trip imaginable.

To those suffering, please sit still long enough to hear the cries from your friends and family and more importantly from God. The noise you create through your addiction and human failing is deafening and from experience I can tell you there are plenty of people who want to help you through this. Let them help you.

There are two things that amaze me through all of this. The fact that my Mom and Dad never stopped loving me and that Jesus Christ waited patiently, for twenty years.

For those of you who are still suffering, I say this: You can't remake your life alone. You need God's help to turn it around. For a long while I thought I'd been abandoned by God but the ugly truth is that I had abandoned God and when I knew I was doing those things that made me ashamed to the core of my soul, I kept telling myself that I could handle anything and everything alone. I made a terrible hell of my life by trying to live without God but when I decided I needed help and asked Him for it, God was there for me. He'll be there for you, too, my friend. All you need to do is ask.

May God bless you in a mighty way!

Epilogue

I fought through dozens of opinions in how, when and what this book should be. At the end of the process, Jack Howard reminded me to just write a story of my life, forwards and backwards, as shaped by my addictions, mistakes, it's selfishness and arrest. Yet, still, somehow, there seemed to be a chapter missing from this first-telling. I knew I had to write my story as someone who had battled from delusion to reality and from anger and addiction to forgiveness and hope.

But make no mistake, it is a battle and a war. In writing a book, you have to finish at some time. And the horror for me in finishing is looking at my life, as it's on these pages, a sum total of things that make me ashamed. The war I have waged has been bloody; the people I have hurt, or even crippled, is so high, that it will take three lifetimes to right the wrongs I have done.

And if I live in ignorance of what I have done, the monster I have been, then I will absolutely do the same things again. To this day, being totally fallible, my temper comes out whenever stress hits me; and most of the time, it's my old habits rearing back. In total honesty, I cannot recall many days since being slapped alongside my head by God that I have not had a rush of anger from my ego ("nobody does anything the way I want!") to my pride ("nobody is as smart as I!"). But I fight like hell to stay in check, holding God's hand with might. I now carry a very healthy fear of me, which ain't a bad thing.

As I am finishing this book, I look at the calendar over my desk. It's taken over a year to get it done so I am fairly happy with it. No, not content; anyone who thinks you can tell an entire life in a book is mistaken. Any single life story is really about hundreds of lives. Our own life, in many levels and also the hundreds of lives tied up inseparably in a million threads. The calendar I am looking at makes me think back over the turbulent year that just passed. One major event was the disgrace and fall of a powerful preacher named Haggard in Colorado. And though our wrongs are so different, I reflect on the fact the sources and outcomes of our wrongs have so much in common. When we hurt someone, we hurt the one we love.

I have been forced to go through help programs: detox, anger management and periodic surprise visits by a probation officer. Many of the rights we take for granted as citizens have been lost to me. Where I go. Who I can talk to. What I can do, eat, or put in my body. All of these things are restrictions now. Unlike many people who complain about losing freedoms, I am pretty realistic about it.

The other problem with telling a story, as an autobiography, is because it cannot be any more true than the awareness of the person who reads it. For example, when I write of being forgiven by my ex-wife, it would be easy for someone who is similarly abusing their partner (and women also abuse men) to simply assume the forgiveness is natural. The deeper truth I have wrestled with here is when I can honestly say my treatment of Cari and thus my children, is really unforgivable. You see, as long as we are talking in the material sense and the physical world, we never really solve what we have done. Once I did a horrible thing to someone, that thing is as real and as permanent as anyone's ability to remember the harm and who may suffer from the evil I did. My unborn great-grandchildren may suffer from the way I have crippled someone.

In a lot of ways, this is because, as a struggling Christian, I have to own up to the things in my heart.

If I can't (or more accurately, won't) confess my ability to wrong others, I will never confront these problems. These tendencies of mine will just lie there, in the dark bottom of my heart and wait for the chance to strike out when the right circumstances come together. This I learned in prison from dozens of stories from people who talked of a sudden temptation. An untested temptation, in other words, doesn't just die from lack of attention.

In every sense of the word, I have committed

almost unspeakable acts. In brutalizing Cari, I have raped her. When a woman offers her man love and he perverts it, their sex is unholy. In cheating others, I have stolen from the elderly; I have betrayed my parents by smearing their good name. By being judgmental, I stop others from achieving their own potential. By mistreating employees, I was cruel to their families.

If there is a limited amount of good in this world, I am one of the devils who have made it this way.

Why is the cost so high when we violate others? Because, as people, we truly cannot ever fix the wrong we did, we can only try to make up for it. We measure this in the most shallow ways we can; as though it's a debt we can count in dollars or on fingers. "Making up" doesn't work that way. We harm people and we do it where we live. And this also means we have to pay twice as high a price. We have to show the ones we hurt that we are for real; and to take a chance on us. Then we have to make sure we don't do the same things again. I don't know about you but most of us can talk the talk, but doing the walk takes something beyond us. We can't make people accept our change. Only God working in us can really heal these kind of breaks.

And finally it came to me there was an element missing from the story about me. The missing part was me. Who had I been during all these years of hell? When the answer came, it also explained some of the missing parts of my story. Most of all, because I realized this missing part is how so many of us define ourselves. As working people, people with jobs. People who go to (or telecommute to) places where we put on our best fronts and try to set a priority on making money.

In my case, I was and still have the heart of a good old-fashioned American entrepreneur. I can't tell the ending of this book, or the beginning of the next part of my life, without facing up to this core set of values and beliefs. After all, it was through these sets of beliefs I justified stealing money and lives and lying to people who would never have hurt me.

An American President once said, "The business of America is business." And for millions of us, there's no fine line between our ethics and our morality. Who we are is typically measured by how much we have. The same applies to religion.

My religion at Healthsphere had room for God, all right, as long as He was a golden God. When things were up on the bottom line, I really felt worshipful! Since losing my own little empire, I have had to reckon what to do about it. My old impulse to get more and be on top is something I have to face. My tendency is to act the same way I have always acted; bully others, mock their efforts and take what I can from the honest efforts of people who mean to help me. Maybe worst of all, I still recoil from people offering to help or when they express worry for me. I am still an arrogant and mean spirited man when under stress. I confess this so God can continue his amazing work in me.

Please don't think I am being needlessly harsh on myself. The deeper facts are the love I have been given makes up for all the things I see wrong in me. And that love is so big it even lets me shake my head at the world's problems. I know this because no matter what happens, I always get stopped and just sense God waiting.

If I turned my back on God's presence, then I would be a shell of a man. I would not live. I would not want to go on living, without His presence. God loved me back to life.

The last thing I want is to sound preachy because I hate being preached to. I figure when it comes to weighing sins, I can figure this out for myself. And as for making people feel guilty, I believe God does that without needing any help. The fact is there's a supernatural presence in my life. My story all started when I was ignorant of it: my guardian angel. I wrote of Crystal, to start this story of my life. It seems right to end with the awe I still feel about Crystal.

Crystal came back to this physical world when my life was going to take one direction or the other. If I had gone to prison without Crystal's angelic intervention, I would have been lost in prison. I would have made a choice to follow more stealing, more pornography, more disrespect towards women and my great love up until then—getting high.

When I was still in prison, I heard an amazing story about angels. And one about demons. This guy was telling about a vision he had, where a demon was whispering to him. The demon said he had the souls of most of a family; all but two of the five family members. This 'demon' said that was enough; that it was time to claim the three souls of those who were the devil's. Pretty weird story. But not the end of the story. Five days after his dream, the whole family died in a fire.

I can't say I have ever doubted since the appearance of my angel's voice, that saved my soul in prison. You might say my angel, my Crystal, makes forgiveness so clear.

please visit
www.godandrodd.org

Acknowledgments

Inside the body of every book is the muscle of memory. In my case, I can only begin to feel the strength of so many friends who have helped pull me back to life.

Jack Howard: Thank you for not resting until this message got out. I will never forget (being the lawyer that you are, you wouldn't let me anyway) how you reacted when Satan hit me with second thoughts. Your belief in this book, skill as a writer and interest in getting me to open up my own deeper story are an inspiration throughout these pages.

Andrea Davis: My dear friend, who read this manuscript over my shoulder for nine months, suggesting things that ultimately lead to better understanding on so many levels. We share a path, so you knew the message from the first day you began reading this manuscript and you pushed me to continue. Without you, I would have quit.

Steve Ormand: I hardly have the words that I feel for all you have done for me. When everyone told you not to hire an ex-con, you did it anyway. Against all odds, you took a chance on me. I will forever be grateful to you. Your grace is beyond comprehension and many could learn true forgiveness in watching your life, though you don't run around professing "I'm a Christian! I'm a Christian!" and your witness is refreshing to people who are tired of being judged or compared. I wrote this entire book on the laptop you gave me since I didn't have the money to buy one. Thank you, Steve O, for never being ashamed of me.

Steve Johnson: My USPO who gave me two choices; either get better or go back to prison. Steve, you were the person in my life who taught me the value of fear. Your amazing ability to 'dial into' most people; street smarts combined with education, is simply amazing. There are so many people in the secular world who could benefit from being held accountable by you. A Christian, a teacher, and a friend.

Gordon (Deacon) and Gail Black: Y'all opened your hearts and home to a complete stranger, moreover, an ex-con. I know it wasn't very long into allowing me into your home that you realized just how big of a project my life was! Nevertheless, you never once wavered in your support and love for me. The only reason this book is complete is because God loaned me Gordon and Gail Black. Deacon, you always considered me your personal project of sorts. Your little brother, huh? You have no idea just how much you have done for my life. Deacon, project well done.

Tommy Nelson: You are absolutely one of the

great theologians of our time. For some reason you never gave up on me. You taught me distance in jogging and more importantly, you showed me the same patience God showed me throughout these years. You have single-handedly informed the entire town of Denton, Texas that the Bible actually has a purpose. It is meant to be read, studied, lived and loved. Since 1988, there has always been a place in your heart for me. I can only say thanks for never giving up on me. You were the first person in my life who, years ago (somewhere between the raid and prison), suggested I should begin keeping a journal. I listened with very sensitive ears and this book is a direct result of that suggestion. You have no idea what you have meant to me over the years. Tommy Nelson, you are a true man of God.

Toby Slough: For giving me and all my brothers and sisters still suffering or in recovery a place in God's house. Your house of worship is one of the fastest growing churches in America simply because you preach from a very broken pulpit. And more importantly, you do not pre-judge, you simply welcome and love mankind just like God does, without walls.

Christina Yulentis: For the months we shared leading up to our respective prison sentences: You will be out of prison soon. Just know that although God has already forgiven you, man will take a minute. Give your entire release and life to God.

LaRue Foster: You realized my journey was getting tough and always gave me words of encouragement and wisdom, as only you can do.

Jody Mabry: You refocused my thoughts mid-sentence. You are a very magical reason why this book is now complete.

Joey Russell: You are an amazing witness and you have led many in Alabama to Christ, not to mention all the others throughout the United States who have benefited and drawn closer to God from knowing you. You absolutely captured the very essence of my life in design and color. Thank you.

Betty Reed (Beethoven): Thank you for opening your home to me in the months leading up to prison. We laughed ourselves silly, especially when you played the piano with only your eyes to be seen over the piano! My goodness, I could hardly sit through church after watching you stomp around like, well, Beethoven!

Lance Reed (Lanny): You were a brother to me in so many ways when I needed a close family. I listened to you talk about the love you still had for your father, who tragically died of natural causes while in prison. You are a true blessing bro'.

Ron Howard: You have a sweet voice that drew me closer to God on so many Sundays.

Jon Rutherford (Boofy): You are a friend to so many. You have been instrumental in my recovery and my life. You are a friend, a true Southern gentleman and a man with all the strength of true gentleness. I hope to learn to be more like you.

Doug Hartman: You have been my hero for so many years. From riding on your shoulders after Bronco football, to entering the healthcare industry together, we had some awesome times! If I were half the man you are, the need for this book would not have existed.

Joe Powell (JP): Thanks for opening your shop to me on so many mornings because I had nowhere else to go before prison. You always had coffee and conversation, and more importantly, friendship. I try to carry and share this lesson now to people that I meet.

Ronnie Anderson, Scott Alagood, and Chris Robinson: You are great friends who I have taken with me throughout my life and will continue to do so.

Everyone at Healthsphere, Inc.: It was so wrong but seemed so right. Y'all were the most incredible employees; regardless of my ill-intentions. I miss all of y'all!

FCI Ft. Worth inmates: Thanks! Glover, we cooked some incredible "throw downs" on those long weekends that will never be forgotten! And D Ray, you always had a Coke and snuff for me, always. Not to mention the fan that saved my life during those miserably hot summer nights.

Al Okler: Though you are now in your own pain, you always had time to listen to me. Your selflessness is a lesson to be learned by so many others. I know your heart has been broken and I feel your pain. You are one of the truly good men in the world.

Dr. Hughs: One of the truly brilliant minds in psychology, who took me from 'Will Hunting,' rebellious, self-centered, self-serving, to seeing the greater good for my life.

(Uncle) Jack Brown: Thanks for taking a chance on me when I was only two weeks removed from federal custody.

(Uncle) Mark Riney: You tried like hell to salvage my company but it was too late, the damage was done. You are a brilliant business man and though things haven't always gone as planned, you never complain. If you ran my company from the get go, I would now be retired in a Caribbean hideaway . . . fishing, relaxing, smiling.

Crystal Pinkston: Your life was taken much too early. Yet, in God's plans, you are so alive in my life! Your death makes helping those addicted or struggling to make sense and to have hope of healing lives. Your Mom misses you every day and this book is the direct result of you. Kenny Chesney sings a song, "You Save Me." It says, "You're the angel that believes in me, like nobody else." Crystal, I am so glad you chose to protect me.

Debi Blagg: (Crystal's mother) Thanks for literally saving my life. You now can see the impact of your single phone call with my dad.

Dixie Hoopes: Thanks for allowing me to share my thoughts with your son, Chris, who is in The Texas Department of Corrections, just two months after my release from prison. And like everything worth having, it wasn't easy. You laid the brick and mortar that began the ministry this book is based upon.

Don Grimes: Your generosity, before and after my time in prison, is the stuff of legends, financially and emotionally. You are a gentle man with very powerful actions.

Stephanie Grimes: The horse whisperer who opened parts of your own heart for the girls . . . whoever invented tough love can say you are a teacher of respect.

Andie Kunik: I hurt you, as someone who loved me truly, gave me children, and stood by me, until I beat you away. You have since showed me more strength, as a survivor of what I did to you.

Mica (my true mini-MeMe) and **Livy** (my 'true lil salesgirl): My little angels who welcomed me back into their tiny worlds, even after I selfishly abandoned their lives. Your little hearts have had plenty of big pains and I need to spend the rest of my life being not only a father but, more importantly, your Daddy.

Shannon and Shari: Y'all deserve more than my simple thanks, for putting up with me, maybe the most self-absorbed, belligerent brother-in-law in North America. I feared the repercussions of my actions would permanently affect a lot of innocents: Todd and Scott, Bailee, Rylee and Kristen, Jordan and Peyton. You both managed to hang in there, holding on to any shred of hope you could find.

Mom: you always showed me love, always. You gave more to me and my life than I could have ever imagined. I am able to write this book and give hope to others still struggling or in recovery simply because you never once gave up on me. The message I send and share with others came from you, Mom. Thank you for standing in my corner even when it meant sacrificing things in your own life. You are a very strong woman, very!

Dad: My whole recovery before prison started with you. We left Denton that morning, terrified. You, because your decision to help me was not a popular one and yet you did it anyway. Me, for surrendering to the demons of addiction, among a long list of others.

You were determined to get your son well again and the last ten years of your life have been just that: your determination for my wellness. While everyone is worried about labels, such as enabler, your love for me is the only thing that you ever cared about. Enabler, you may have been but, nevertheless, you absolutely saved my life through your endless and amazing love.

Scott: My older brother and the family patriarch; thank you so much for the hard lessons learned. You taught me very tough love and it is finally beginning to pay off. You taught me that things worth having take time, patience, hard work, dedication and that nothing comes easy. When everyone in Denton had their share of me after Katrina, they chose you to do the dirty work. That was the best and hardest thing that has ever happened to my life; it was finally rock bottom. We both cried that morning. You, for giving me one choice: leave Denton, now! Me, for wondering if my life was truly for naught. And on Christmas, two months later, you called and left a message on my mobile phone that keeps me motivated daily. You said, "I'm proud of you Rodd. Keep it up!" Your words were slurred as you fought back your pain and emotions. Scott, you are a role model to so many but, more importantly, to me.

Todd: You are my best friend in the world, my buddy for life, my gift from God, my soul mate from birth, my twin. You spent one year reshaping my thoughts, convincing me of a potential that Satan had nearly taken. "You can make it!" "Don't quit on me now!" "Hang in there boy!" among many other one-liners that made me both cry and laugh. Your words in my ears on many mornings gave me strength. Funny, you would spend well over an hour quoting the Bible (true to your DTS roots), preaching, teaching and sharing. Inevitably you asked, "Now you don't think I'm preaching to you, do you?" Of course I did, but please, preach on 'lil buddy! Your presence in my life changed my days.

Mom and Dad, your parenting, Todd and Scott, your brotherhood, for those years could be an inspiration for parents, brothers (and even sisters) who feel at the end of hope. All your hard work has a reason: no matter the mistakes I made, your love and teaching has been the steady candle in my dark night. Though I made so many years so very hard, and the tears were heavy, I thank God that the hard part is finally behind us.

And most of all, **Jesus Christ**, first and last, my Lord and Savior, who reached into a life filled with utter chaos. A place where self-destruction was mind-boggling. Jesus dusted me off, smacked me across my head and sent me on the most incredible journey I could have ever imagined.

Printed in the United States
82292LV00001B/1-12